An Atheist and a Christian Walk into a Bar...

An Atheist and a Christian Walk into a Bar...

Talking about GOD, the UNIVERSE, AND EVERYTHING

RANDAL RAUSER and JUSTIN SCHIEBER

Prometheus Books
59 John Glenn Drive
Amherst, New York 14228

Published 2016 by Prometheus Books

Cover image © nednapa/Shutterstock
Cover design by Liz Mills
Cover design © Prometheus Books

Inquiries should be addressed to

Prometheus Books
59 John Glenn Drive
Amherst, New York 14228
VOICE: 716–691–0133
FAX: 716–691–0137
WWW.PROMETHEUSBOOKS.COM

20 19 18 17 16   5 4 3 2 1

Library of Congress Cataloging-in-Publication Data

Names: Rauser, Randal D. | Schieber, Justin, author.
Title: An atheist and a Christian walk into a bar... : talking about God, the universe,
    and everything / by Randal Rauser and Justin Schieber.
Description: Amherst : Prometheus Books, 2016. | Includes bibliographical
    references and index.
Identifiers: LCCN 2016029166 (print) | LCCN 2016033689 (ebook) |
    ISBN 9781633882430 (pbk.) | ISBN 9781633882447 (ebook)
Subjects: LCSH: Christianity and atheism. | God (Christianity) | God.
Classification: LCC BR128.A8 R38 2016 (print) | LCC BR128.A8 (ebook) |
    DDC 261.2/1—dc23
LC record available at https://lccn.loc.gov/2016029166

Printed in the United States of America

*Randal: For all those who ever cried out,
"Lord, I believe; help my unbelief!" (Mark 9:24).*

*Justin: For all those who once wished for an audience with the divine
only to be met with an utterly indifferent cosmos.*

CONTENTS

ACKNOWLEDGMENTS

Randal and Justin would like to thank their editor, Steven Mitchell and the rest of the team at Prometheus, who caught the vision of this book and have carefully shepherded it through to completion.

Randal also wishes to thank his wife and daughter for their enduring support, as well as his beloved parents, who raised him into the faith he still holds. Thanks also go to Randal's dogs—Maggie the chubby Maltese and Sonny the emotionally detached Lhasa Apso—for providing comic relief and the welcome daily opportunity to pick up some poo in the backyard. Finally, a nod must go to the humble HP Pavilion on which Randal typed his share of the manuscript: you may not be the coolest laptop, but you get the job done.

Justin wishes to thank his *Reasonable Doubts* comrades Jeremy Beahan, David Fletcher, and Luke Galen. Thanks also go to Alexander Delorme and the University of Alberta Atheists and Agnostics, as well as Yorgo Veenhuyzen, for organizing a debate between Randal Rauser and himself that served as the catalyst for this project. Thank you to Jennifer Beahan, Ed Brayton, Jeff Seaver, and the rest of the gang at the Grand Rapids, Michigan, chapter of the Center for Inquiry. Thanks also to Brandon McCleary, Jeff Lowder, and Hasan Mohammad for their friendship and encouragement.

INTRODUCTION

RANDAL'S INTRODUCTION

In October 2005, Jon Stewart, the former host of *The Daily Show*, appeared on CNN's *Crossfire*, a debate program that regularly pitted a strident conservative opinion against an equally strident liberal opinion in a no-holds-barred, no-compromise-allowed, debate.

But this episode wasn't merely another conservative vs. liberal dispute. Instead, Stewart proceeded to eviscerate the format of the show, arguing that it encouraged polarization while distorting complicated issues in favor of simplistic sloganeering and partisanship.

These days, debates on God's existence are often carried out in the manner of *Crossfire*, with theistic and atheistic apologists each aiming to demonstrate the truth of their position while showing their opponent to be not only wrong but plainly irrational or even morally suspect. It is not uncommon, for example, for atheists to denounce theists (and in particular Christians like myself) as *faith-heads*, a derogatory term popularized by Richard Dawkins. Alas, many Christian apologists respond in kind, as they attribute the atheist's unbelief to sinful rebellion against God.[1]

Irrational faith-head theists and sinful, rebellious atheists. As if these are the only options? Yikes!

Indeed, "Yikes" doesn't quite convey how damaging this kind of marginalizing rhetoric is. The reality is that atheism and theism are both intellectually serious, rationally defensible positions. Each position is supplemented with dozens of arguments that have been ably defended by many of history's great minds (and more than a few less-than-great minds as well!). And if we are to have any hope of learning from one another on this most important of questions, we had better start by learning to listen, even as we continue to argue our points with conviction and charity.

13

That's what this book is about. Justin and I may find ourselves at opposite ends of the God question, but we respect each other and acknowledge that we are bettered by serious exchange with those with whom we disagree. We're not attempting to reinvent the wheel in this book. But we are attempting to polish the rim and try on some new tires. In short, we're aiming to provide a helpful model for rigorous and charitable intellectual exchange. Along the way, we also hope to defend some important arguments in favor of our worldviews.

You may have noted that I referred above to both theistic and atheistic apologists. Alas, the word *apologist* often has negative connotations today, as if an apologist is little more than a glorified used car salesman who is merely interested in closing the sale.

Needless to say, I have no interest in *that* kind of apologetic. The Greek word *apologia* refers first and foremost to a formal defense of one's beliefs. And what could be wrong with that? But while I definitely resonate with that pursuit, I also believe that one should only defend one's beliefs because one believes them to be *true*. This means that I view apologetics as a quest for truth. And if we're really serious about that, then apologetic debate should be as much about revealing weaknesses in one's own views as illuminating their strengths, for if our views fail to match up to the truth in any way, we should want to know. Serious dialogue is a fantastic testing ground for our beliefs in the manner of iron sharpening iron.

For this reason, in one of my books I define apologetics as "the rigorous pursuit of truth in conversation."[2] The fact is that I believe I am right to maintain that God exists, and Justin believes he is right to maintain that God does not exist. But above all, I believe we should both be committed to pursuing and knowing the truth, and a conversation that is friendly, rigorous, honest, and directed at the truth reflects and embodies that commitment.

With that in mind, my hope (dare I say my *prayer?*) is that this conversation can help us in that journey. If God exists, Justin wants to know, and if God *doesn't* exist, I want to know.

So let's get started!

JUSTIN'S INTRODUCTION

When my family left the Catholic Church in which I was raised for a church in another part of town, I wholeheartedly approved. Not only were the services of our new evangelical Protestant church adorned with occasional distorted guitars and drums, the man at the helm was less than two hundred years old. I viewed this as a clear improvement.

It was around this time that I allowed myself to begin taking Christianity seriously. I began playing worship music for the various youth programs and dove deep into what I believed to be the Word of God. Prompted by my noticeable enthusiasm, I was approached by one of the youth pastors and encouraged to take the next step—baptism. I wanted to. I really did. But I took the invitation so seriously that I wanted to be absolutely sure that I was ready for an honest commitment to Christ. It was roughly six months later that I eventually did experience the power of water-based human rituals. I came out of that water before the entire congregation and, more importantly, to the cheers and tears of family and friends. It was a profound experience.

To the dismay of my parents, this religious high didn't last another year. Doubts slipped in and grew like an unchecked cancer. I'd always believed that the claims in the Bible were *spiritually true,* but at this point I was having an increasingly difficult time thinking that the events to which the texts referred were real events that happened on earth to persons like you and me. Also difficult for me was squaring the concept of love with certain divine actions and commands attributed to the character of God in the Bible. When the most violent text you read as a child is that of your religious, theistic tradition, it can induce a moral confusion with the power to stain your entire web of beliefs.

Moreover, the silence on the other side of my prayers, which, up to that point, I had interpreted as God intently listening, was now just that—a deafening silence. I called out. I heard nothing in return. I fought like a good Christian soldier to preserve what little confidence I had in the truth of Christianity, but I lost that battle.

However, I never fully lost interest in the topic. Since the rejection of Christianity doesn't entail a rejection of theism, and since theism is a much simpler hypothesis than Christianity, I wanted to know if theism had any substantive intellectual merit. To learn the answer to my question, I decided that I needed to hear from the best critics and defenders of theism. I therefore dove headfirst into the deep waters of academic philosophy of religion in my spare time. This was the better baptism, a renewal of an entirely different sort.

Undergoing dramatic changes of worldview can be a frightening and exciting time. For me, coming to believe that I had been profoundly wrong about things of which I once felt certain birthed a kind of struggle in me. On the one hand, it humbled me epistemically. What *else* could I be so profoundly wrong about? On the other, it ushered in a brief period of arrogance and condescension toward persons of religious belief. In my experience, this is a common phase for many who fail to maintain the religious faith of their childhood. I eventually grew past that sad attitude. Books like this are what can happen when persons of two opposing sides work to mature past stereotypes and oversimplifications in an effort to uncover even just a portion of the rich philosophical landscapes surrounding one of the biggest questions: the existence of God.

Chapter 1

WHY GOD MATTERS

Randal: Justin, thanks for agreeing to have this discussion on God, the universe, and everything.

Justin: Randal, you're very welcome. I'm always up for meaty conversations on big topics with interesting people.

SHOULD YOU CARE IF GOD EXISTS?

Randal: And I'm always up for meaty conversations with folks who think I'm interesting, so this could definitely work!

As you can guess, since I'm a theologian I'm always interested in talking about God. But I admit that a lot of people don't share that interest. About a decade ago, Jonathan Rauch coined a new term, *apatheism*, in order to describe his attitude toward God. The word was a portmanteau of atheism and apathy. As you can guess, Rauch's point was basically that he doesn't care whether God exists or not.

Justin: Yes! I've heard that before and, well, I must admit to being a sucker for a good neologism.

Randal: Yeah, me too. (Although I admit that I was less impressed when Bill Maher came up with the term *religulous*, a portmanteau of ridiculous and religious.) Anyway, these days I find a growing number of people share Jonathan Rauch's attitude. They may call themselves atheists, but at an even deeper level they're apatheists. They may believe God doesn't exist, but more fundamentally they *don't really care* whether God exists or not.

Justin: I certainly have come across people with similar attitudes toward God and religion. One interesting thing about Rauch's concept of apatheism is that it can be found on all sides. Rauch writes that apatheism is "a disinclination to care all that much about one's own

17

religion, and an even stronger disinclination to care about other people's."[1]

Here he uses the word *religion* broadly to mean any belief system—theistic, atheistic, or other. For example, you can have a disinterested atheist who, for whatever reason, just doesn't care about the concept of God. You can also have a disinterested theist who, while believing in, say, Christianity, never bothers to read the Bible or attend church on any regular basis.

Randal: Good point. Apatheism is an attitude you can find across the spectrum of professed belief. In fact, I've met more than a few apatheists who attend church regularly. Apparently it's just what they do. But it doesn't seem to change anything in their lives. It's merely perfunctory, a matter of inertia. Those folks are sometimes called *practical atheists*. They may accept Christianity, but for practical purposes they might as well be atheists because they don't live out the beliefs they profess.

But apatheism isn't just a matter of failing to live out your beliefs. After all, no Christian fully lives out the beliefs they profess because no Christian is exactly like Jesus. At its core, apatheism within the church is found in a broad indifference to theological belief and spiritual discipleship. Within this context, apatheism might manifest itself in a religious commitment that reduces Christianity to a Sunday morning self-help seminar where God is a mere life coach who wants us to have (in the words of Joel Osteen) our "best life now."

Justin: Right. For example, self-identified Christians might be less interested in the big points of their theology and more interested in the more common moralistic aspects. It could be seen as a kind of weekly moral therapy.

Randal: Yup, the First Church of Apatheism!

Justin: These churches resemble social clubs more than they do places of worship. It's an interesting phenomenon, to be sure. Though, if I might ask, what do you think lies behind the religious apatheism?

Randal: A good question, and a complicated one too. For starters, I think one must identify the growth of secularization. The word *secular* comes from a Latin word meaning *world*. So a process of secularization is a process by which folks become less focused on matters of God, religion, and spirituality, and more focused on everyday mundane matters. To be sure, this isn't necessarily a bad thing. After all, life is about balance. Not even the most spiritually attuned person can live 24/7 with her head in the clouds. But once your religion is limited to a Sunday morning pep talk, it's hardly surprising that religious indifference becomes the norm.

Justin: That makes sense to me. It's a kind of a reorienting of cultural priorities. As a secularist myself, this is just par for the course. Given that we are sharing the same planet, any reorienting of religious attitudes toward more practical, ground-level concerns is certainly something I endorse.

Randal: I hope you'll forgive me if I'm not *quite* as enthusiastic about secularization as you are! If you view secularization as clearing the air, I view it potentially as a build-up of smog that prevents us from seeing the sky.

Justin: Ah, I have to disagree with the implication that an increase in, or a reorientation toward, the world must serve as a kind of smog polluting our view of our proverbial sky, which I take to mean a sense of awe. In fact, learning the very real processes of science can be a huge source of awe and empowerment. For me personally, the notion that I am connected in a very real, biological way to every living being on this planet is capable of bringing with it a crippling sense of awe at times.

Randal: Cue "The Circle of Life" from *The Lion King*! But seriously, I share your awe at the natural world. I'd just say that my awe doesn't stop there.

Anyway, lest I get sidetracked, let me come back to your question about religious apatheism. There is another factor evident in my view. In fact, I think this factor drives both Christian and secular apatheism. I'm thinking here of the perceived irrelevance of theological questions for daily life. There's an old chestnut that describes the discourse of academic theology as equivalent to debating the absurd and irrelevant question, "How many angels can dance on the head of a pin?"

Justin: Twelve.

Randal: Huh? Twelve *what?*

Justin: That's how many angels are capable of dancing on the head of a pin at any given time! Try to keep up.

Randal: Ahh, I need to run to keep up with you! (Although I disagree with your answer: since angels have no spatial extension, the right answer is an *infinite* number!)

Justin: More seriously, I admit to viewing some theological questions similarly. I worry that those doing theology are too often building elaborate and detailed conceptual cathedrals to make their observations fit their basic theological commitments, but they so rarely question those core commitments in the first place. But I agree that this is no reason to dismiss considering the God question in a serious philosophical way.

Randal: Got it. However, many Christians will say the same thing about sophisticated accounts of naturalism, the philosophy most commonly associated with atheism these days. That is, they'll accuse the naturalists of building elaborate and detailed conceptual cathedrals to make *their* observations fit their basic metaphysical commitment, that is, the commitment that *nature*, whatever that turns out to be, is all that exists.

Justin: That's certainly fair.

Randal: Of course; I'm always fair!

Personally, I don't see a problem either way. It seems to me that we all start with a set of assumptions, and as we seek to understand the world in light of those assumptions we craft a theory that will accommodate all the data. To those who don't share our starting assumptions, the whole endeavor can look like an exercise in painting the target around the arrow. But the fact is that everybody needs to start somewhere. We all need to begin at a particular starting place and reason from there. And where we start will determine how we go forward.

Justin: I can agree with you here. I just don't think that this entails that all conceptual cathedrals are created equal. Some conceptual cathedrals really are much more ornate and detailed than others.

IS GOD AS RIDICULOUS AS AN INVISIBLE PINK UNICORN?

Randal: True. And by the way, some defenses of naturalism are *very* ornate, decked out with the metaphysical equivalent of Corinthian columns and flying buttresses.

But hey, I'm heartened that you agree theism is an intellectually serious position. If you didn't, this conversation would probably be a lot shorter!

At the same time, I regret to report that not all atheists agree with you. Indeed, these days I regularly find belief in God being dismissed as the intellectual equivalent of belief in an invisible pink unicorn or a flying spaghetti monster or garden fairies. Apparently the idea is that a Christian's belief in the Trinity is no different from a child's belief in Tinker Bell.

Justin: In the case of the unicorn, I'm always left puzzling over exactly what shade of pink is compatible with being invisible. I suppose that their point could be that the concept of God contains a contradiction, in which case their efforts would be better served by providing an argument to that end. Cartoonish assertions don't exactly deserve much by way of response.

Randal: Yea and amen to that. I can't count how many times I've met an atheist who thought merely comparing theism to something wacky like the flying spaghetti monster was some kind of rational trump card: "Bam! I win!"

So does that mean that you don't find *any* contradictions in theism?! (Fingers crossed!)

Justin: I suppose I should have been clearer here. I think there are some significant problems for the coherence of theism. Sophisticated incompatible-properties arguments are no small part of the literature in philosophy of religion, but I'm not yet convinced that an air-tight case against theism can be found among them. Often these properties (omniscience, omnipotence, omnibenevolence, etc.) just need a bit of tinkering in their definitions in order to get them to fit together conceptually. Whether or not these ad hoc defenses of theism's coherence are indicative of a less-than-noble approach to these issues is a different question.

Randal: Fair enough. Where the invisible pink unicorn is concerned, I agree that the surface target is the alleged contradictions involved in theological constructs. The Christian ponders how God can be one and three. And the devotee of the invisible pink unicorn ruminates on the mystery of a unicorn that is both invisible and pink.

Justin: Let's not forget Homer Simpson's famous knock-down theological challenge, "Could Jesus microwave a burrito so hot that he himself could not eat it?"[2]

Randal: Yeah, that's a real brain buster! Believe it or not, I use Homer's question as an illustration when I lecture on the divine attribute of omnipotence to my seminary students.

But if apparent contradiction is the surface target of the invisible pink unicorn meme, I suspect that the ultimate or deep target is the credibility or intellectual seriousness of theological enquiry itself. Just as we would dismiss any sophisticated philosophical defense of an invisible pink unicorn or a flying spaghetti monster as absurd, so the objector dismisses any defense of the Judeo-Christian God.

Justin: Right. These points can seem rhetorically powerful but, in my opinion, fail to say anything interesting.

Randal: I do think these objections at least reveal something interesting about the objector's attitudes. It seems to me that the point of comparing God to whimsical beings like fairies, leprechauns, the Easter Bunny, and Santa Claus is more specific than merely poking at the alleged absurdity of theism. In the case of these particular comparisons, I suspect the point is to suggest the arrested intellectual development of theists by comparing God to a fanciful belief from childhood. So it goes like this: there was a time when most children believed in beings like Santa Claus, but when they grew up they put away childish things. Likewise, when people are ready to grow up intellectually, they put away the childish belief in God. So theists are like Linus still clutching onto his baby blanket.

Justin: Unfortunately, you're probably right about that. Some people actually believe that no intelligent adults are capable of holding theistic beliefs. And, well, let me be unequivocal in saying that, not only do these people have a profoundly simplistic understanding of human psychology and the ways we form beliefs, but their theory is pretty much destroyed by the evidence of many adult theists at all levels of intelligence.

Randal: That's for sure. Just to underscore that important point, consider the case of Aksel Hallin. Dr. Hallin is the Professor and Canada Research Chair for Astroparticle Physics at the University of Alberta. In the 1990s, he was on a team working at the Sudbury Neutrino Observatory, and the work of that team was recognized in 2015 with a Nobel Prize. As it turns out, Dr. Hallin is also a member of my church. I know many brilliant adult Christians like Dr. Hallin. But I've never met a brilliant adult who believed in Santa Claus, let alone an adult believer in Santa who occupied a research chair in physics.

So the differences are glaring. And that raises the question: why do you think these caricatures persist among atheists?

Justin: Hmm, good question. One reason for their persistence might be that unsophisticated ways of justifying theistic belief are popular and very much related to having an unsophisticated concept of theism. Atheists living among theists with unsophisticated methods and concepts will likely be addressing the same unsophisticated concepts.

Randal: So, if I understand you, the idea is first that people who have a simplistic understanding of God also tend to have a simplistic grasp on how to justify their belief in God. And second, when atheists are regularly exposed to those simplistic theists, they respond in kind with simplistic caricatures of their own making. Is that the idea?

Justin: Yes, I think that's right.

It seems to me that people in such situations are likely to place the implications of the existence of God on a par with the implications of the existence of Santa or anthropomorphic spaghetti dinners. Granted, this is more of a psychological explanation of these attitudes rather than an attempt to justify the reasoning that led to them, but I think that's what we're after.

Randal: Got it. I agree that some popular Christian conceptions of God are ripe for the parodies that one finds among some atheists. For example, picture the Christian who prays for a good parking spot at the shopping mall on Saturday. I can understand how the idea that God intervenes in the space-time continuum to secure parking spots at the Pottery Barn for his cherished bargain-seeking, upper-middle-class suburban followers leaves Christians ripe for some parody.

Justin: A target-rich environment to be sure. Though, to be fair, it's a bit more understandable if we're talking about finding a parking spot on Black Friday down here in the States.

Randal: Granted, that *would* be evidence of divine intervention.

Justin: But, more seriously, I think it also has to do with the literature of the tradition to which they belong. According to Matthew 7:7, a part of the Sermon on the Mount, Jesus is recorded as saying, "Ask, and it will be given to you; seek, and you will find; knock, and it will be opened to you."[3]

You may disagree with their interpretation or that it applies to parking spots or football games, but we can hardly blame them for a straightforward reading.

Randal: Actually, I *can* blame folks for this kind of simplistic proof texting, this taking isolated verses out of context. In any case of interpretation, whether of the Bible or any other text, we should try to avoid extracting individual sentences from the contexts in which they are embedded. That said, I think a careful reading of Jesus's words in context precludes the common shallow and self-serving interpretations to which you refer. His promise applies to the selfless pursuit of God's kingdom, not the selfish pursuit of discounted material goods at suburban shopping malls.

Regardless, you're right to point out that this kind of simplistic, self-interested reading is not uncommon in the church. The problem, as I see it, is that too often atheists make the leap from parodying some crude form of Christianity or theism to parodying theism itself. And that's where the atheist gets into trouble because you don't judge an idea by its weakest examples. That's nothing more than the strawman fallacy, in which a position is rejected based on weak exemplars of the position.

Justin: It's certainly true that hasty generalizations are *never* wise.

Randal: Never *ever*? Wait a minute. Did you just make a hasty generalization? Heh heh.

Justin: I was wondering if you were going to catch that one. Well done.

HOW DO YOU DEFINE *GOD*?

Justin: It seems to me, then, that before we can make a case for the importance of the question at the center of this book we should say something about what we mean by *God* here.

Randal: Excellent observation. Here we are, engaged in a conversation of God with no definition yet on the table!

Justin: For various reasons, both historical and philosophical, not all God concepts are taken equally seriously. In the Western world, at least, it's classical theism that reigns supreme.

Randal: I think you're right that in academic discussion classical theism is the go-to definition and the one we should assume as well.

That said, I suspect not everybody knows what classical theism is. Nor should we assume that we mean the same thing by it. Heaven forbid we should waste any time talking past one another. So let's start here: how do *you* define classical theism?

Justin: At least as I've understood it, classical theism assumes a non-physical agent (God) who is omniscient, omnipotent, and perfectly good. Now, as we've already hinted at, the precise nature and implications of these attributes leads to some disagreement among theologians. Once one aspect is clearly defined, it may have inescapable effects on attributes elsewhere. But, at least for now, noting these basics should suffice.

Randal: I agree with your working definition, so far as it goes. But perhaps I can unpack it a bit more.

As you point out, God isn't a physical thing, and so he is not made of matter. Note that I just referred to God with the male-gendered pronoun *he*. Let me hasten to add that this does not mean that God is more like a man than a woman. Rather, this is a reflection of the limitations of English, which lacks a personal nongendered pronoun. (The impersonal gender-neutral pronoun *it* is not a good option when referring to God because we don't refer to a person as *it*, and in classical theism God is a person.) So while I will refer to God with male-gendered pronouns, we can just treat that as a linguistic convention, one which is borne of the limitations of the English language.

Justin: Well, I would argue that the tendency to use the male-gendered pronouns when referring to God is not *just* a limit of language.

After all, in the literature for the Abrahamic religions (Bible, Qur'an, etc.), God is usually referred to with male-gendered pronouns. Somebody of that tradition could hardly be blamed for assuming that God is a male because God is seen as a *father* rather than a *mother*. These patriarchal assumptions within the literature will unavoidably influence the institutions built around them. In the Catholic Church, priests are referred to as *father*, whereas women are not permitted to take on the priesthood. But, even if a gendered view seems suggested by some theistic traditions, it is certainly not necessary to the core concept of theism.

Randal: Okay, but there is plenty more data to consider before we conclude the biblical portrayal of God is patriarchal. For example, keep in mind that Genesis 1:26–27 teaches that men and women are equally made in the image of God. Man is *not* more godlike than woman. Moreover, the Bible includes many descriptions of God in female, and specifically maternal, terms, as in Deuteronomy 32:18 and Isaiah 66:13. I will agree that unfortunately the church has often downplayed these important female and maternal themes. But if we keep them in mind they definitely help counterbalance the tendency toward patriarchy.

Justin: To shake up the cultural assumption of God as a male, I often will use female-gendered pronouns.

Randal: Fine by me. Shake all you like!

Anyway, one thing that is clear from this discussion about pronouns is that God is understood to be a person or an agent. It's worthwhile saying a bit more here, too. For God to be a person/agent means that God has a mind, he's conscious, and he can act with intentions or purposes.

You also described God as having three great attributes: he is omniscient (all-knowing), omnipotent (all-powerful), and omnibenevolent (perfectly good).

Justin: Right. Well, at least as God has been traditionally defined.

Randal: Yes, and I agree with all that. But let me add one more important point. We also want to keep in mind that God is a *necessarily existent being*. In other words, God could not fail to exist. Philosophers and theologians sometimes describe this property as independence or aseity. This means that God exists *in himself.* There is nothing outside God to explain his existence.

While I don't believe you can find all the divine attributes in the Bible, I do find divine aseity suggested, if not clearly taught, in several passages. Consider, for example, Paul's words to the Athenians as recorded in Acts 17: "The God who made the world and everything in it is the Lord of heaven and earth and does not live in temples built by human hands. And he is not served by human hands, as if he needed anything. Rather, he himself gives everyone life and breath and everything else."[4]

It's really important to underscore necessity or aseity in our definition because it reminds us that God is the end of the explanation. When folks miss this fact, all sorts of confusion can result. For example, I've often heard atheists object to the notion of appealing to God as the explanation for the existence of the universe by retorting, "What caused God?" But that kind of objection is a complete misfire because it shows the objector doesn't understand that the cause being invoked is necessarily existent. If God exists, it makes no sense to ask what *caused* God.

Justin: It might also be worth mentioning here that many atheists, myself included, also believe themselves to be committed to some form of a necessarily existing *stuff*, whatever that might be. One reason for thinking this is that absolute nothingness in the philosophical sense seems like an impossibility. If that's true, then *it is necessary that something must have always existed.* For largely the same reasons as you've expressed above, these atheists view questions like "*Why is there something rather than nothing?*" as confused.

Randal: Hmm, I'm not sure I agree with you that those things are equal. There is a fundamental difference between thinking, as you do, that *some kind* of substance exists in every possible world and thinking, as I do, that one particular substance, *God*, exists in every possible world. Agreed?

Justin: That is true.

Randal: Okay, so then let's summarize our definition going forward so we can finally get into some rip-roaring debate. We've agreed that God is a necessarily existent nonphysical agent who is omniscient, omnipotent, and perfectly good. That certainly doesn't say *everything* a theist will want to say. But it is good enough for our discussion to get going.

Justin: Okay, great. If that's the definition of God we're going with, I will, for the remainder of our exchange, define atheism as the belief that there is no God. I also want to supplement this definition, for the sake of our exchange, with the additional claim that there are no *other* supernatural entities capable of creating or otherwise interacting *within* the natural world.

Randal: Good point. So now that we've got some definitions down, where do you want to begin?

WHAT ABOUT AN EVIL GOD?

Justin: Now, Randal, we seem to be in agreement that this traditional view of theism is the view that gets the most attention. Obviously, there are various other views ranging from polytheism ("There are many gods") to pantheism ("The totality of existence is identical to God"). To be sure, I think there are good reasons to take seriously the traditional view of theism over these other views of theism. That said, are there any reasons, besides historical contingency, for this focus on considering the traditional view of God over, say, a God that is identical in every way but, instead of being perfectly good and loving, is perfectly evil?[5]

Randal: No offense, but I find the question confused, not unlike the "What caused God?" query. As Anselm famously observed, God is *by definition* that being than which none greater can be conceived. In other words, God is the greatest or most perfect being one can imagine. Needless to say, any concept of maximal greatness or absolute perfection includes *moral* perfection. This is absolutely essential to the idea of God in classical theism. Since we've agreed to work within the limits of that idea, the question "Why not think of God as perfectly evil?" really cashes out to "Why not think that a devilish maximally evil being—a being with the greatest amount of evil imaginable—exists instead of God?"

If one of us believed a maximally evil being exists, it would make sense to debate the reasons to believe such a being exists. Since neither of us believes in a maximally evil being, I think we can set that fanciful entity aside and get on with the discussion of God. Is that fair?

Justin: You're certainly right that the traditional definition of God involves moral perfection. But I want to get *prior* to that. If the quibble here is just on the use of the word *God*, then that's fair. I guess I don't see a problem with entertaining non-Western views of God. It's true that neither of us believes in such an evil being, but that seems irrelevant to my question. My question is *why* we should take that traditional view more seriously than a view that suggests a maximally evil being.

Randal: I think you're missing the point that the topic of a debate is determined by the views the participants think are plausible options for belief.

Look, let's turn the tables and imagine that the focus of our debate is naturalism rather than theism. In that case, we're going to start with a mainstream definition of naturalism to which you're committed and go from there. You'll then present arguments that favor your thesis and I'll present arguments against it. At the same time, that requires us to set aside literally dozens of competing definitions of naturalism. But that's the way it is: if we don't do that, we'll never get started.

I'm not interested in defending pantheism, polytheism, henotheism, Manichaean dualism, process theism, or maximally evil beings. I take it you aren't either. So we can set all those concepts aside and get to the topic we both think *is* a worthwhile debate, namely classical theism vs. atheism.

Justin: It would definitely be crazy to expect us to address such a broad swath of ideas about the divine. We are but mere mortals!

Randal: True. Although people are often awestruck by my presence, I am indeed a mortal.

Justin: However, there are reasons we might want to examine the maximally evil being vs. God question. For example, nearly every argument that might be used to support the God hypothesis seems to provide equal support for the maximally evil being hypothesis!

Randal: Hold on a minute! I need to challenge your claim that "nearly every argument" supports the existence of a maximally evil being as readily as God. For example, arguments from moral value, moral accountability, moral obligation, and aesthetics clearly *don't* support the existence of a maximally evil entity.

Justin: While arguments *for* a traditional God using moral value, accountability, obligation, and aesthetics wouldn't strictly support a maximally evil being, a *mirrored* version of each seems perfectly capable. I suppose an example might help. An aesthetics argument that focuses on the amount of beauty in the world might support traditional theism to some degree or other, but an argument from the amount of ugliness in the world could support the maximally evil being hypothesis. See what I mean?

Randal: I understand what you're thinking, but I don't agree that you can create a "mirrored version." If you're going to defend that claim you first need to provide an ontology that is, an account of the nature, of *ugliness*. On one mainstream view, ugliness is not a thing that needs to be explained. Let me give an analogy: the existence of light needs a source or explanation, but darkness doesn't need a source (or explanation) because it is merely the absence of light. Similarly, if ugliness is understood to be merely the absence of beauty, then the existence of ugliness *doesn't* need an explanation parallel to the existence of beauty.

Justin: But that's my point!

Randal: Huh?

Justin: These are the kinds of Western theological assumptions we should at least be wary of. The idea that ugliness is merely the absence of beauty or goodness is a cultural assumption. It's no more plausible than its mirrored version that states that beauty is just the absence of ugliness!

Randal: I don't think we're tracking with each other here. I'm saying that you *can't* create a mirrored version because, on the definition I provided, aesthetic value is an existent thing that requires an explanation, but the *lack* of aesthetic value (in other words, ugliness) would not be an existent thing that requires an explanation. So your attempt at a mirrored argument supporting a maximally evil being doesn't work if one accepts this mainstream account of aesthetic disvalue (or ugliness).

Justin: Right, I'm just noting that there seems to be no essential reason to prefer this view over its opposite. The arguments certainly don't favor one over the other.

Randal: Well, I don't think we're in a position to make that judgment yet since we haven't begun to weigh the respective arguments for various theories of the nature of beauty and ugliness.

Regardless, at most all I see you doing here is pointing out the fact of *underdetermination*. (The term underdetermination refers to cases where the available evidence is not sufficient to justify a particular conclusion. For example, the fact that the driveway is wet *underdetermines* the conclusion that it is raining because the driveway could be wet due to other causes, like a sprinkler, for example.)

Christians are well familiar with this fact of underdetermination. After all, most arguments for God underdetermine the truth of specifically *Christian* theism (and thus, they could also be used by Muslims, Jews, and deists). So it isn't surprising that some of those arguments might also underdetermine the truth of classical theism in such a way that they are consistent with your maximally evil being. That's no problem for the theist, but it is a problem for atheism, and that's what you need to worry about.

By the way, the same point would apply if you were defending naturalism. In that scenario, much as I present an argument consistent with several versions of theism, so you could present an argument that would be consistent with several distinct versions of naturalism. But given that I reject *all* versions of naturalism, what *I* should be concerned about is the extent to which that argument contradicts theism.

Justin: That's true. Notice though, that the move from one form of naturalism to another is a relatively minor move, while the move from classical theism to the view that a maximally evil being exists is an impressive metaphysical chasm.

Randal: I disagree. Metaphysical chasms divide naturalistic theories as well. For example, one view of naturalism says all that exists are material atoms in a void. Another view of naturalism, on the other hand, says that reality also includes conscious minds and even an eternal, immaterial, Platonic good. Yet another view says that naturalism makes no claims about what exists *at all* but instead only addresses what can be known or what kind of knowledge is preferred (i.e., scientific or empirical). There are some formidable gaps separating all those views.

Justin: Granted. I just think it's interesting that classical theism gets all the attention, while the claim that a maximally evil being exists gets practically none at all, especially since they seem to enjoy the same support and neither is more complex than the other. This difference in air-time strikes me as more cultural than logical.

Randal: I don't think they have the same support. For one thing, I've already given you several examples of arguments for God's existence that would not constitute evidence for the existence of your maximally evil being. If you are really serious about defending the existence of this supremely malevolent creature, you should be writing another book since, last I checked, this book is devoted to debating theism.

The bottom line is that evil-being theories get no attention because nobody holds that a maximally evil being exists (unless, of course, somebody believes in the devil and believes the devil is that maximally evil being). It's really that simple. Once again, if you want people to take evil-being theories seriously, you need to present arguments for the view and win people over to it.

Justin: Perhaps you're not as bothered by this as I am. For you, being a theist, it makes sense that an Evil God is not something you have much reason to think about. But for myself it's not that easy. I'd like some reason other than culture and history to take classical theism more seriously than a maximally evil being.

Randal: And you can apply that same point to naturalism. If you're a naturalist, there are countless *versions* of naturalism you never consider seriously. And the limitation of culture and tradition is a big factor in which views you consider possible options. The fact is that whatever your views about the nature of the world, there is an infinite number of competing theories that you ignore without a second thought. That's true of everybody, not just the theist.

And let me add one more thing: from a Christian perspective, the fact that we naturally form beliefs in a good God rather than a malevolent being is not merely a matter of culture and tradition. Rather, we naturally form beliefs about God because we believe we are *designed* to function in this way. In other words, belief in God is natural, it's hardwired, while belief in a maximally evil being is not. So if a person is a theist they *expect* that belief in God would naturally arise and so be more common than belief in a maximally evil being.

Justin: I understand.

Though, it's worth noting that, while beliefs *consistent* with traditional monotheism are *natural* in the sense that they are very intuitive and easily acquired, those same beliefs are *more* consistent with animism and polytheism.

Randal: Yeah, that's true. But the critical question is whether careful reflection on these naturally forming beliefs in a god of some sort is best explained by the deity as described in classical theism. I believe it is.

Anyway, how about we move on, with my promise that I will discuss some moral arguments that explicitly support the existence of God rather than some evil being?

Justin: That's fair. Don't let me forget to bring it up!

Randal: You have my word.

But it looks like you still have something else you want to say. Speak up man! There are no secrets here!

A DEBATE ABOUT MERE (CLASSICAL) THEISM

Justin: Right, well, at this point, I think it's very important that we make it clear that theism as we've defined it says nothing about an afterlife, be it pleasant or dismal. It also says nothing about any grand salvation narrative and it doesn't suggest any metaphysical law that states that the spilling of blood has redemptive powers. These are certainly popular beliefs in the Western world, but they are better seen as cultural additions. One can be a theist in the sense we're using here without being a Christian or an adherent to any of the other major Abrahamic Faiths.

Randal: That's a really important point. All those additional topics you mention certainly are worth discussing (though I wouldn't simply describe them merely as cultural additions). Bottom line: those doctrinal claims are not a part of *this* discussion. We're debating the existence of God here. We can set specific theological particulars aside for another day.

And, by the way, perhaps I can add that this point works for atheism, too. These days folks often lump the rejection of God in with a rejection of all sorts of other things: ghosts, crystals, ESP, mediums, dowsing rods, near-death experiences, and who knows what else. But our concern here is simply with God, not every belief you might encounter at some esoteric occult convention.

Justin: I think that's a good point. It's important to keep the concepts relatively bare on both sides. There are certainly atheists and theists on all sides of other metaphysical questions, but we shouldn't unfairly burden everybody in a group with these assumptions.

Randal: Exactly. We should always be careful about the baggage of added assumptions. For example, I'm Canadian, but don't assume that means that I like hockey (I don't) or that I'm polite (I'm not, especially in heavy traffic).

As for the popular association between atheists and the rejection of crystals, ghosts, and dowsing rods, the idea, presumably, is that the same skepticism that leads a person to reject God will lead them to reject all these other things. And that's fair enough; I get that. But we should keep in mind that one can be an atheist and still believe in things like dowsing rods and an afterlife. Granted, that might be surprising, much like a rude Canadian who doesn't care for hockey. But it isn't impossible.

So, as we proceed, let's just focus on that biggest of questions: God. We can set aside our heated debate on dowsing rods for another day.

Justin: We agree. One of my favorite philosophers, J. L. Schellenberg, writes, "Our job as philosophers, faced with the question of God's existence, is to fight free from the distractions of local and historical contingency, to let the voice of authority grow dim in our ears, and to think for ourselves about what a God and a God-created world would be like."[6]

Randal: Hmm, without wanting to nitpick here, I find myself saying *yes* and *no.*

Okay, I admit it: I *do* want to nitpick.

Justin: Pick away, Randal.

Randal: On the one hand, I say *yes,* where possible we should look into matters for ourselves. This reminds me of the spirit of the European Renaissance, which was captured with the famous Latin phrase *ad fontes,* meaning "back to the sources." In other words, don't just give in to tradition. Don't just accept something because everyone else does. Take a look and discover for yourself.

That sentiment also gained pivotal significance in the Enlightenment. Immanuel Kant made the point in his famous 1784 essay, "What Is Enlightenment?" where he challenges the reader to use their own reason.

That spirit of individual inquiry applies to the study of the natural world, of course, and there we find the seeds being sown for modern science. And it's also what drives people to think about theological and philosophical questions without falling back on tradition.

Justin: I can agree here.

Randal: And yet, I also want to add a *no*, or at least a serious qualification to the *yes*. I fear that Schellenberg is a bit too hard on those voices of authority. My point here is that sometimes we can be naive and cavalier as we reject the long-established wisdom that has gone before us in favor of what just seems to us to be right.

It seems to me that it's all about balance. We should be willing to question and look for ourselves, but we should *also* be willing to consider carefully the well-established positions that come before us, for there is a lot of wisdom in the past. And to borrow a phrase from Isaac Newton, if we can see far it is only because we stand on the shoulders of giants.

Justin: That's true. Though, I think Schellenberg is not suggesting we outright dismiss prior conclusions, which themselves have been culturally reinforced over time. Rather, I read him as expressing the importance of being mindful of how cultural assumptions can sometimes inject bias into our investigations, possibly even preventing us from asking more fundamental questions. I think we can agree that *that* is something to avoid.

Randal: I hear you! I'm reminded of the story of one particular Crayola crayon. Up until 1962, that crayon was labeled *flesh* color.

Justin: Oh, boy. That's awkward.

Randal: Heh, yeah. Then pressure from the civil rights movement led Crayola to relabel that color *peach*.

Looking back, it's hard to believe how people could have failed to see how offensive and patently ridiculous it would be to label *one* color of crayon as *the* flesh color. But it just didn't seem that obvious in the 1950s. That's a valuable lesson for us all as we ask to what degree does *our* cultural background and limited experience shape the way we see the world? And where do we need to critique those assumptions?

Justin: Absolutely. These are all essential questions for those interested in examining their own beliefs.

SHOULD YOU HOPE THAT GOD EXISTS?

Justin: Well, it seems we've now defined how the words *theism* and *atheism* are being used in this book, but we haven't yet addressed specifically *why* the question of God's existence is one of significant weight. Why should we bother?

It seems to me that if, for the sake of the argument, we assume that God exists and has created finite creatures[7] (like those whose eyeballs are following this line of text), then there exist benefits *potentially* available to us that would *not* be available if God did *not* exist. Here I refer to the increased access to moral goods, particular kinds of profoundly spiritual and life-changing experiences, and the occasional divine helping hand. There are perhaps other benefits as well.

Randal: I agree that God's existence would make a difference in terms of providing goods for creatures that would not otherwise be available. But God's existence would not only produce goods relative to the well-being of creatures. It would be a good in itself. Indeed, by definition, God's existence would be the very greatest good possible. After all, God is defined as a maximally good being.

So I'm guessing that whatever differences we have, we agree that, if the God of classical theism exists, then that would be an extraordinary fact.

Justin: Indeed. It's always nice to start with some common footing.

Randal: Yes sirree. But not only is the question of God important, I think it also follows that we ought to *hope* that God exists.

Justin: Ah, but Randal, that's not immediately obvious to many.

Randal: You're right about that. In the last decade, I've found it increasingly common to find atheists stating not just that they don't believe in God but that they *hope* there is no God. Ironic, eh? At the same time that some atheists are yawning their way into apatheism, others are raising a closed fist to the very idea of God.

Justin: Yes, that's certainly a view that's found some footing. Philosopher Thomas Nagel famously wrote, "I hope there is no God! I don't want there to be a God; I don't want the universe to be like that."[8]

These atheists who hope there is no God often refer to themselves as *antitheists*.

Randal: Yes, not to be confused with the *Auntie* theist you visit every Thanksgiving. (Sorry, bad joke.) But seriously, antitheism is quite common these days. Indeed, in some camps it seems like atheism and antitheism are pretty much considered one and the same thing, so that atheism involves *hoping* God doesn't exist as much as it involves *believing* God doesn't exist.

Christopher Hitchens (may he rest in peace) used to love comparing God to a despot like Kim Jong-il of North Korea. For Hitchens, living under God would be living under cosmic tyranny. So, not only did he believe God didn't exist, he also hoped he was right, and he was prepared to rebel against any God that should appear on the scene.

Justin: Very true. For Hitchens, the wish for God to exist was the wish to be a *slave.*

In a 2008 debate with his brother, Peter Hitchens, Christopher proclaimed the following:

It [a desire for God to exist] is the desire for an unalterable, unchallengeable, tyrannical authority who can convict you of thought-crime while you are asleep . . . who must indeed subject you to total surveillance around the clock, every waking and sleeping minute of your life, before you are born and even worse, and where the real fun begins, after you're dead. A celestial North Korea. Who wishes this to be true? Who but a slave desires such a ghastly fate?[9]

Beyond the master/slave rhetoric, which I think is without merit,[10] there exists, I think, a legitimate concern about theism. If theism is true, it does rob us of any sense of privacy. Our thoughts are not our own. So, while I agree that, all things considered, we have more to gain if theism is true and so should prefer that be the case, this is one issue that seems to bring at least some support for the opposite conclusion. Would you agree, Randal?

Randal: That reminds me of the story of average guy Alex Moss. When he was remodeling his bedroom, Mr. Moss found the following note hidden in the fireplace: "Hello, welcome to my room. It's 2001 and I am decorating this room. Hope you enjoy your life. Remember that I will always be watching you."[11]

Always watching?! Brrr. Moss thought that was sufficiently weird to share the story online. And it quickly went viral, as people reflected on how creepy it would be to have somebody always watching you. So I get where you're coming from.

Having said that, let me answer your question. No, I don't agree with the objection as applied to God, because it seems to be based on a crude anthropomorphism. That is, it arises from the error of uncritically thinking of God in human terms, as someone like the mysterious voyeur who formerly lived in Alex's bedroom.

An invasion of privacy occurs when another agent surveils your actions, as in a peeping Tom peering through your blinds or a secretive government agency listening to your phone calls or reading your emails. But God's knowledge of us is nothing like that. God doesn't surveil your actions. That is, *God doesn't gain new information about his creatures by surreptitiously observing them.* Rather, as a necessarily omniscient being, God simply knows all true statements from eternity. Since God's knowledge of us has no relation to the peeping Tom or secretive government agency, the suggestion that God invades our privacy just strikes me as confused.

Justin: Hmm. I can agree with you that you've identified a difference between God's knowledge of all events and typical cases of human knowledge. But why should we think that distinction is of any relevance? For it seems to me that, however the knowledge is gained, the fact that our thoughts are not ours alone still remains and that fact should at least count for something.

Randal: What do you mean "our thoughts are not ours alone"?

Justin: Simply that we cannot be alone with our thoughts. With theism, we lack all privacy of mind.

Randal: It seems that your language gains in poetic panache what it loses in analytic precision. To be frank, I'm still unclear why you believe that a necessarily existent being's knowledge of all true propositions constitutes an invasion of your privacy.

Let me try a different angle: A few years ago, I learned that there are tiny creatures, creatures that are too small to be seen by the human eye, that live on the human forehead.

Justin: Gross.

Randal: That's what I said!

Justin: What are they?

Randal: Unfortunately, finding out the answer didn't make me feel any better. *Demodex* have eight legs and long chubby bodies, and they live their entire lives crawling around near our eyebrows. At first, this revelation was so repulsive to me that I had to fight the urge to dip a hunk of steel wool in bleach and go to work on my forehead.

But lo, over time I've grown accustomed to the idea of those critters living on my forehead. If I can get used to the prospect of something as unsettling as bugs living on my face, I think you can get used to the prospect of a morally perfect, necessary being knowing all true propositions from eternity, including whether you will have pastrami on rye for lunch next Tuesday.

Justin: I'm not claiming that it would be perpetually terrible if God were to exist. Remember, I still think it would be a good thing, *all things considered*, for God to exist. I am simply claiming that this is at least *one* reason, however small you think it is, to wish that God didn't exist. The fact that I could get used to it after a while doesn't negate the fact that it is one relevant factor.

I might get *used* to the fact that a neighbor can hear me making love, but I may *still* think of this as a reason for preferring they didn't live on the other side of the wall!

Randal: Once again, you're falling into the anthropomorphic trap of envisioning God taking in knowledge about his creatures through some kind of external perception. But it's not like that. God doesn't observe us by hearing or seeing what we're doing through a wall. God does not surveil us to gain knowledge of us. That's not how omniscience works.

Anyway, the reason I brought up the point of getting used to *Demodex* living on my forehead is to illustrate that in retrospect my initial revulsion at these creatures was misplaced. In fact, they don't impinge on my enjoyment of life, and it just took some time to realize that fact.

Similarly, I think that once you recognize that God isn't the North Korean despot of Christopher Hitchens's imagination, you can likewise see that a divine being's knowing all true propositions from eternity is not, in itself, ground to worry about an invasion of one's privacy.

Justin: Sure, I'm merely claiming it's one factor but is outweighed by other concerns. So, even though you may think of Hitchens's privacy complaint as irrelevant, I think it carries *some* weight. That said, Hitchens was wrong to conclude that, *all things considered,* the wish for theism to be true is no different from the wish to be a slave.

Randal: We definitely agree on *that* point.

Chapter 2

GOD, FAITH, AND TESTIMONY

Randal: Now that we've got some preliminary points out of the way, perhaps we can dive into a particular topic. I want to come back to the point you raised about unsophisticated defenses of theistic belief leading to ridiculous caricatures like the flying spaghetti monster. So, if it is okay with you, perhaps we can shift gears from talking about the concept of God and attitudes toward God to the rationality of *belief* in God, including the questions of faith and knowledge.

Justin: You'll get no protest from me.

GOOD AND BAD FAITH

Randal: Cool. You certainly are an obliging chap!

Okay, so you drew an important link between unsophisticated approaches to justifying one's belief and the problem of blind faith. At this point, skeptics often raise an objection to fideism, the belief that faith need not depend on evidence. With that in mind, I want to make two points in response.

First, while fideism can provide a poor or unsophisticated response to the question of justifying belief, that isn't necessarily the case. In other words, appeals to fideism can be sophisticated and worth taking seriously. For example, Christian philosopher Robert Merrihew Adams defends a form of fideism in his essay "The Virtue of Faith."[1] And many other Christian philosophers have done so as well.[2] You might not agree with their approaches, and that's fair enough. But hopefully we *can* agree that fideism can be *sophisticated* even if we might disagree about whether it is *right*.

Justin: Sure, I can agree here. It may be fair to call some views of faith

41

sophisticated in the sense that their ideas are clear and complex, even if I ultimately remain unmoved by their efforts.

Randal: Okay, good. And second, I'd want to add that just as fideism can be sophisticated, so the *denial* of fideism can be *unsophisticated*. Indeed, in my experience very often it is.

Justin: Hmm, could you elaborate?

Randal: But of course. For example, I can't count the number of times I've heard atheists say things like "I always believe based on evidence." As popular as that mantra may be in some particular circles, it's simply an absurd claim, and it's also demonstrably false.

Justin: That's right. To take a classic example, that individual likely believes that the external world exists—that there is a real, physical world that exists *out there* that they are indeed perceiving. And yet, what evidence could they possibly bring to the table to demonstrate this?

Randal: Yeah, that's a big problem. As every philosopher knows, providing evidence for a physical world is not as easy as most folks think. After all, much of that so-called evidence is perfectly compatible with the scenario in which there is no external world and we are minds in a matrix being fed sensory data to create the illusion of a physical world.

Evidentialism is the idea that one must have evidence for a claim to be justified in believing it. These days, naive versions of evidentialism are common, according to which this justifying evidence must be scientific or at least empirical. Consider, for example, the person who says, "If I can't experience it with my senses, then I won't believe in it." In my opinion, the naive evidentialist who believes she can justify all her beliefs with evidence is a fitting complement for the crude fideist who refuses to justify any of his beliefs. Here we have two equal and opposite errors.

Justin: I share your concerns here about some of my fellow atheists or anybody who would venture to assert that *all* of their beliefs are based on evidence. That's a pretty naive view. My concern lies primarily with fideism in its most egregious form, which I believe we both agree is problematic.

Randal: Not so fast, bub. I agree that some forms of fideism are problematic (just as I suggested that some forms of evidentialism are problematic). But I'm not sure that you and I *do* agree on exactly what a problematic instance of fideism would be. Can you give an example of what you're thinking? What does that look like?

Justin: I think we do (or perhaps *should*) agree that, as a general rule, an attitude or approach to faith that discourages investigation is problematic. I dare say this should be uncontroversial.

Randal: Hmm, I'm not so sure. Can you unpack that some more?

Justin: Consider a young man picked up by the police late one night for allegedly committing some heinous crime or other. His family is notified of his arrest, but their faith in their son is so great that they confidently conclude there must have been some mistake.

A short while later, the family members of the accused show up to the trial proceedings for support. However, when it comes time for the prosecution to make their case, the family dons earplugs and eye-covers to preserve the strength of their trust in him. Despite the evidence piling up, they choose to stay headstrong in their faith. Once the defense begins their case, the family promptly removes their headgear and listens intently.

Randal: What? That's outrageous!

Justin: To be sure, this is an extreme example for illustrative purposes, but I've had my fair share of conversations with people who pridefully and unapologetically view their faith in an analogous way. It's quite common actually.

Randal: That may be as you say, an extreme example, but things like that *do* happen. In my book *You're Not as Crazy as I Think*, I give a real-life example along those lines.[3] In that case, two brothers were plotting to kill their parents for the life insurance money. The FBI was tipped off to the conspiracy and launched an investigation. As part of that investigation, an undercover agent posing as a hitman had a conversation with one of the brothers about planning the hit. The exchange was recorded and later played at trial, but *the parents refused to listen to the recording*. In short, they popped in those ear plugs you described. All the while they resolutely maintained that their beloved boys were set up.

As a parent, my sympathies are with those parents. I can't imagine how painful it would be to learn that your children wanted to kill you! But from a rational perspective, their refusal to consider the evidence before them was indefensible. Theirs was a bald case of choosing to maintain comforting self-deception over the cold, hard truth. And I agree that this is fundamentally irrational.

Justin: They were certainly guilty of the crime of irrationality, but, wow, that must have been tough to hear.

Randal: Tell me about it. The ultimate betrayal!

I guess the additional point I'd like to make is that I see people *across the spectrum* engaging in this kind of behavior. It certainly isn't limited to those who would describe themselves as religious. Self-described skeptics, atheists, and humanists can also act this way.

Justin: Your addendum is noted and appreciated. In my experience, the community of those who self-identify as atheists or skeptics are very fond of and very skilled at *communicating and promoting* the values of skepticism and critical thinking. However, communicating those values is one thing and putting them into practice is quite another. Like any other community united around some core ideas or beliefs, we too can quite often fail to embody those values—especially in our interactions with outside groups or individuals.

Randal: I appreciate you saying that. It reminds me of the unfortunate relationship Christians frequently have with grace. While we Christians talk a lot about grace, it's one thing to talk grace and quite another to embody the values of grace in one's life. When it comes to matching our behavior to our beliefs, we're all works in progress to some degree.

DEFINING FAITH

Randal: Okay, that's enough mea culpas for now. Perhaps we can switch gears at this point and turn to defining *faith*. Just as there are many different definitions of God, so there are many different definitions of faith. In particular, there are two basic ways the word faith is defined, and they are often conflated in discussions like this. So it's probably worthwhile to be clear on the distinction.

Justin: That's a good point. That word gets thrown around a lot, and it's not always clear what usage is intended.

Randal: In the first sense, faith is roughly equivalent to religion. Insofar as we are working with that definition of faith, it's clear that some people have faith and some don't because some people are adherents to a particular religion, while others have no religious affiliation.

Justin: Right. As with the phrase, the *Abrahamic Faiths.*

Randal: Yup. In this sense I've got a faith (Christianity), but you don't.

And in the second sense, faith is roughly equivalent to *trust.* In other words, to have faith in something is to trust in that thing. If I have faith in the truth of a proposition, then I trust that the proposition is true. If I have faith in a person, then I am inclined to trust what this person says as being true. If I have faith in my cognitive faculties, like sense perception and memory, then I trust that the deliverances of these faculties are generally reliable.

Justin: That makes sense.

Randal: I think it's important to make this distinction clear because I often hear those without a religious faith (the first definition) insist that they don't have faith in something like the second sense. But this is simply false. Whether you have a religious affiliation or not, everybody must still trust in some truth claims, in particular persons, and in the very cognitive faculties that mediate information about the world to us. There is no view-from-nowhere that allows us to test our beliefs apart from faith. So only some of us have faith in the first sense but *everybody* has faith in the second sense.

Justin: I suspect that the nonreligious community would rather use trust than faith when speaking of confidence in some proposition or person because of faith's religious connotations. But it's certainly the case that the word can be used in both senses.

Randal: While some folks may feel better about using the word trust, the truth is that there is nothing especially religious about the term faith. Just listen to George Michael's 1987 hit song "Faith," in which the pop star's call to have faith is focused on a lowbrow desire for sexual contact with a woman. Needless to say, there are no lofty religious convictions in *that* use of the word.

The lesson is that the very common tendency to pit faith against reason is wholly mistaken, for reason always begins in faith or trust.

This reality goes straight back to our earliest formation as infants and toddlers, as we extended trust to our caregivers to mediate information about the world to us. Indeed, I like to describe faith and reason as the two oars of a boat. If you only row on one side of the boat, you go in circles. You need faith and reason together to advance in your understanding of the world.

Justin: Thank you for that important distinction. A core takeaway here is that, whatever word we might prefer to use when talking about confidence—be it faith or trust—not all confidence is equally rational.

But, at this point, I'd like to make a related and important point: the rationality of one's *faith* or *trust* in, say, the goodness of a person, the usefulness of an idea, or the accuracy of a text can exist in degrees that can change over time.

In the case of the parents who turned a blind eye to the incriminating evidence against their two sons, they had *faith* or *trust* in their children's innocence. It might be the case that their trust was the rational result of consistent saintly behavior from the two brothers until the night in question. If it were, their faith in the innocence of their children was well-placed, given the information to which they had access at the time.

Where they erred was not in their original faith or trust in the innocence of the defendants. Rather, their mistake was when they let this supreme confidence in the innocence of their sons get in the way of updating their current belief with important additional information from the prosecutor.

FAITH IN THE MESSINESS OF LIFE

Randal: Yup, and this is one of the places where I think folks often get into trouble when judging the rationality or objectivity of other folks. The problem comes when we judge the rationality of other people based on the set of beliefs *we* hold. That's a mistake.

Justin: I agree, and it's a very common mistake. The question is not whether or not some particular belief is rational, the question is *rational for whom?* Some beliefs can be rational for some persons but irrational for others.

Randal: Right. And this is a point worth underscoring with an example, one that brings us squarely back to theism.

Let's say, for example, that Pastor Jones prays for his daughter to recover from a bad case of pneumonia. A couple hours after the prayer, the daughter begins to show dramatic signs of improvement. By the next day, she is fully recovered, and Pastor Jones concludes that God healed her.

I have often heard religious skeptics reply that this kind of interpretation of the recovery is irrational because the child's improvement could just as well be due to chance. I agree that it *could* be chance: nobody's denying that. However, we should also remember that Pastor Jones starts out with different background beliefs from the skeptic. Pastor Jones believes there is a God who answers prayer, while the skeptic doesn't believe this. Since they have different starting points, each reasonably interprets the same data differently relative to their background assumptions. As a result, the pastor can see the hand of providence while the skeptic sees mere serendipity.

So here is how this cashes out: it is reasonable for Pastor Jones to attribute the recovery to divine action, and it is reasonable for the skeptic to attribute it to chance. The point is that we don't need to decide which interpretation is reasonable or justified. Rather, Pastor Jones and the skeptic can *both* be reasonable in interpreting the data differently, each in accord with his background beliefs.

Justin: Well, I certainly want to join you in agreeing that the beliefs we hold prior to confronting new data can greatly affect our interpretation of that new data. But allow me to look closer at the example you've provided here before we move on.

Randal: I'm fine with that. My examples are not cheap knockoffs. They tend to look even better on closer inspection.

Justin: It's certainly true that it would be irrational for the skeptic to believe that God is the cause of the healing, because he doesn't even believe that God exists! On his view then, such an event would be impossible. Moreover, an event like this isn't going to constitute significant evidence of the sort that might change the skeptic's mind. But the pastor . . .

Randal: Whoa, hold on there, comrade. An interjection is required. I agree that it would be irrational for the skeptic to attribute the miracle to God while *continuing* to believe God doesn't exist. But that's very different from a scenario where the skeptic *comes to believe God exists based on the evidence of the putative healing.* And I don't see any problem in principle with that.

Justin: Okay, so that addresses the skeptic, but what about the pastor? This is the more interesting question of the two, or at least it seems so to me. Obviously, the pastor believes that God exists and that God is *capable* of answering prayers. For the pastor then, God's answering his prayer by healing his daughter's pneumonia is not logically ruled out by his preexisting beliefs. But, just because they are not ruled out by his beliefs, doesn't necessarily make his *conclusion* that God has answered his prayer rational.

Randal: Granted it doesn't follow automatically. But what makes you think it would not be rational?

Justin: As a pastor, he has undoubtedly prayed before. In fact, he has probably prayed much more than the average congregant.

Randal: One might hope.

Justin: How many of those prayers in the past have been answered?

How many haven't?

What *counts* as an answered prayer?

If he prays for healing for a friend and his friend suffers for another ten years before experiencing some healing, does that count? Clearly the pastor thinks that *some* prayers might come true even if God wasn't the cause of their coming true. Given these heavy complexities, of which the pastor will be aware, I doubt that even he is going to be within his rational rights to attribute his daughter's healing to the God he believes in.

Randal: Okay, I see where you're coming from.

My problem with what you've said here is that you can raise similar problems with inductive knowledge *generally*. In deductive reasoning, the premises follow necessarily from the conclusion, but in inductive reasoning the premises only make the conclusion more likely. And yet, while we all appeal to induction, it raises deep philosophical problems.

For example, how do we justify drawing general conclusions based on a limited selection of examples? And how do we justify making assumptions about the future, such as that the sun will rise tomorrow, based on a limited experience in the past? And how do we justify a belief in the uniformity of nature? And then there is the *new* problem of induction raised by philosopher Nelson Goodman, which I don't even want to get into here because it will end up taking us down a rabbit trail.[4]

The bottom line here is that induction raises a nest of problems every bit as complicated as the problems you've posed for the pastor. And yet we all appeal to induction. I think a good lesson is that we should begin by addressing general problems with knowledge in areas like induction as a preface for discussing specific examples of problems like the pastor's belief about answered prayer. Moving in that way, from the general to the specific, ensures that we're being consistent rather than applying standards to others that we don't apply to ourselves.

As for me, the lesson I would draw from the pastor's case is simply that questions of rationality, evidence, and belief are contextualized to particular individuals in particular contexts with particular beliefs. And we need to be careful about judging the rationality of others based on the set of beliefs we hold.

Justin: I think you're right in that we should be careful about judging the rationality of others based on the beliefs *we* currently hold. Remember, I argued specifically from the beliefs the pastor has and not from the beliefs I have. It isn't at all obvious that his theistic belief, which makes answered prayer possible, is even remotely sufficient to justify his conclusion that God *answered* his prayer. Simply pointing to old philosophical controversies about induction doesn't give your pastor a free ride to conclude anything he wants.

Randal: The disputes about induction aren't "old." They remain live issues in academic philosophy. And I didn't suggest the pastor gets a "free ride" or that he can "conclude anything he wants." His belief arose naturally in response to an apparent instance of a fulfilled request. And I think that conclusion is perfectly reasonable given the unusual recovery, the context in which it occurred (following a prayer), and the pastor's background belief (God sometimes, but not always, responds favorably to requests for healing). Raising broad issues such as you have isn't sufficient to establish the irrationality of his belief.

If you really want to talk about free rides, then it seems that we're *all* getting a free ride in the sense that we form beliefs through induction even though we haven't rebutted every serious objection to induction. And if that is the case, then why pick on the pastor?

Justin: I pick on the pastor because of the *nature* of the claims being made. Pastor aside, we seem to be in agreement then that, as a general rule, an attitude or approach to faith that discourages investigation is problematic. Perhaps it might be of some value to briefly touch on what an exception to such a rule might look like?

FAITH IN YOUR SHERPA

Randal: This may be a quibble, but I don't think we should speak of exceptions to the rule, if the rule is construed from the outset as a general rule. For example, if the general rule is that vehicles on the road should observe the speed limit, the ambulance that exceeds the speed limit while driving a critically ill patient to the hospital is not *violating* that general rule. Rather, the ambulance operates within it, for *the general rule allows precisely these kinds of exemptions.*

Justin: You're right about that. My mistake.

Randal: Similarly, if we accept the general rule that it is good and proper to be ready to question or investigate those things we trust, we could still recognize instances where it is advisable not to do so.

Here's an example of what I'm thinking: You're a city slicker climbing Mt. Everest guided by an expert Sherpa. In that circumstance, your survival depends on absolute and unqualified trust in your guide. The fact that radical trust (or faith) is required in that instance doesn't *violate* the general desirability of a critical mind, just as a speeding ambulance doesn't violate the speed limit.

Justin: I'm afraid I need to express some hesitance toward your example here. It seems to me that, if all we know about the Sherpa is that they identify as a Sherpa, it hardly justifies an unqualified trust in them as a guide. This is especially true in such a high-risk situation. I can easily think of situations where their decisions would best be met with a heavy dose of skepticism.

Randal: Ahh, I can tell you've got something in mind that you want to share. Do tell!

Justin: Let's say you're ten days into your journey up the mountain when you realize that you are rapidly losing daylight and the temperature is dropping faster than expected. Let's also say that you've just arrived at a seemingly perfect camping spot and the journey ahead looks to be particularly treacherous for several hours at least.

Randal: Hmm, sounds like an ideal place to stop! Time to make some s'mores on the fire.

Justin: Right! So, then if your Sherpa guide *insists* that you press onward, unqualified trust in their plan would seem reckless given the high-stakes nature of the situation. At the very least, you should ask them to inform you of the details or reasoning behind their plan for pressing on into the cold. Perhaps their expertise gives them insight into the terrain not immediately available to you, but the risk is too great to follow your guide's plan unquestioningly. After all, what if your guide is new to this route or new to being a guide altogether? Maybe they've forgotten something. Experts aren't infallible.

Randal: You're right about that last bit. To err is human!

On the other hand, if, as I said, you're a city slicker, and this Sherpa has shown himself capable during the previous ten days of hiking, then I would be inclined to think your decision to disregard his advice at this point *would* be foolhardy. Keep in mind as well that "Sherpa" is a vetted and elite status like "Texas Ranger" or "Navy Seal." As a result, generally speaking, any person who has attained the status of a Sherpa warrants your trust.

And it isn't hard to imagine things that Sherpa might know that you don't. For example, it could be that this clearing that seems so inviting to you is prone to avalanches, rockslides, or attacks by the Abominable Snowman.

Justin: Yahhhs!

Randal: Sorry, I didn't mean to scare you. Sometimes I don't realize my own power as a storyteller.

How about this: perhaps the Sherpa knows of a sheltered cleft in the rock just over the next ridge that offers a safe respite from the elements.

Justin: Ah, but remember, never did I advocate disregarding the Sherpa's advice out of hand. I've only suggested an inquiry into the *details* of the Sherpa's plan. At that point, he might be able to share a new bit of information with you, like your sheltered cleft, which might make his decision seem less suicidal from your point of view.

If, however, we were talking about a fast-paced decision where there wasn't time to ask about the Sherpa's reasoning, it would probably be best to side with the Sherpa.

Randal: *Now* I'm on board with you.

Justin: Attaboy, young Padawan.

Randal: Yes, I'm glad you accept the wisdom of having *faith* in the Sherpa.

Justin: Trust!

Randal: Faith, trust, whatever you prefer!

And, since I'm a big fan of give-and-take, I'll happily give a little by acknowledging that such faith is not *absolute*. In other words, there are limits to our deference to the Sherpa's authority. For example, I would think that if the Sherpa advised you to take a hunk of granite and start hitting yourself in the head, you'd be wise to demur. Faith does have its limits.

Justin: I'll say!

Randal: At the risk of following a rabbit trail, at this point I can't help but think of Hugh Thompson Jr., a helicopter pilot with the US Army during the Vietnam War. On March 16, 1968, Thompson was ordered to provide air support to the ground operations that were seeking to flush out Viet Cong soldiers. But, to his horror, Thompson gradually realized that the ground soldiers were carrying out a massacre on the civilian population of the village, a slaughter that would later become known as the infamous My Lai Massacre. Despite the fact that Thompson was ordered to fire on the Vietnamese villagers, he refused to do so. In my view, Thompson was a moral hero who recognized that his faith in his commanding officers was not absolute.

So I heartily accept the caveat that evidence can arise that will lead the rational person to withdraw support for a person or a belief. That's a really important point. But I think we also need to recognize the extent to which each one of us extends trust (and thus faith) to others. This isn't simply something the religious do.

And that brings us to the big question: when is it rational to do so?

Justin: Right. *All* belief systems exercise trust, whether they're secular or religious. We all exercise trust in the behavior, advice, and promises of authorities, lovers, and friends.

So, when is it rational to exercise trust in other persons? That's a question I have a few ideas about but no simple, final answer. I'd definitely say that there is some value in a demonstration of consistently good character, either through your personal history together, by the testimony of a trusted friend, or through an institution with some reliable vetting capabilities. There is always the possibility of a situation where we have no choice but to trust another person.

Randal: The truth is that I could talk about Sherpas all day. But I suspect it is time to tie this general discussion of faith squarely back into the question of God's existence. We defined God earlier as a necessarily existent nonphysical agent, who is omnipotent, omniscient, and perfectly good. Thus far we have also said something about having faith in Sherpas and other human beings.

Justin: There's that damn Sherpa talk again.

Randal: Sorry, I didn't realize it was a sore spot for you! Okay, no more Sherpas, at least for a while.

The next question concerns what it would mean to have faith in *God's* existence. And I think the place to begin is with faith in testimony.

Fortunately, it isn't hard to find additional examples where we exercise faith in the testimony of others. We trust teachers, friends, neighbors, family, weather forecasters, authors, and so on. Day by day we have faith in the testimony of a bewildering number of people, at least provisionally.

If we can believe all sorts of other things based on the testimony of others, it would seem we could also believe in God in this manner. In other words, one way to have faith in God would come through the testimony of fellow theists as to God's existence and nature. To be sure, I don't think testimony is the *only* way one might reasonably believe God exists. But it would seem to be one way.

What do you think?

THE PRINCIPLE OF TOTAL EVIDENCE

Justin: You say that the testimony of others seems like one way by which one might reasonably believe in God. I interpret this statement as being about evidence—that it's at least possible for testimony to serve as *some* evidence for God. I must presume that you do not mean to say that mere testimony is always sufficient for reasonable belief in God. After all, concluding that God exists merely because of some testimony seems flawed, since it would violate the Principle of Total Evidence.

Randal: Principle of Total Evidence, eh? Sounds important! Can you define that?

Justin: According to Elliot Sober, the Principle of Total Evidence is "just the idea that we should use all the evidence we have to evaluate the hypothesis at hand."[5]

So, then, it seems to me that the question is whether or not I think testimony can constitute *some* evidence for the existence of God. Is that fair?

Randal: If I follow you, you object to the possibility that one might reasonably believe in God by way of testimony because you believe this person wouldn't have considered *all* the available evidence. Did I get that right?

Justin: What I mean is that, *if it's true* that one is *not* considering all the available evidence for and against God, then their conclusion that God exists is premature at best. Would you agree?

Randal: That's an interesting claim. Of course, this cuts both ways, so one should likewise withhold belief in God's *nonexistence* until considering *all* the evidence. From that, it follows that atheism could not be a rational default position.

Justin: I would agree.

Randal: Glad to hear it because many atheists today argue that atheism *is* the default position.

But setting that aside, let me raise two related objections to your claim or at least to how one might cash it out.

First, it seems to me that the Principle of Total Evidence, such as you've defined it here, is demonstrably false.

Justin: Now, wait just a minute!

Randal: I know, that seems harsh, but hear me out. Let's say that I get a call from my friend in London. "What's the weather like right now?" I ask. And he replies, "It's raining."

Simple, right? Common sense would say that his testimony provides an adequate basis to believe reasonably that it is now raining in London.

Justin: Okay.

Randal: But not according to your Principle of Total Evidence.

Justin: Hmm. I'm not sure I follow you.

Randal: After all, there is much more available evidence to consider, including the testimony of all the other people presently in London, satellite data, inferential environmental cues (e.g., the present dampness of the ground in London), and so on. There are all sorts of additional evidences I *could* consider.

Despite this fact, it is also clear that I *can* reasonably believe it is raining based on my friend's testimony, without surveying all this other data. In fact, it would be *unreasonable* to withhold belief until I had surveyed *all* the evidence. And so, the Principle of Total Evidence, as defined, is false.

Justin: Okay, I think I see what has happened here. I'll respond in a second, but maybe you should tell me your second objection before I do so.

Randal: Right, so back to it. Second, let's turn to your belief in the Principle of Total Evidence itself. Have you comprehensively surveyed all the data relevant to the truth or falsity of that principle, including a thorough engagement with the expansive field of philosophical epistemology that would be relevant to the evaluation of the principle? If you haven't, then your acceptance of the principle violates the principle.

Having said all that, I agree that there is a commonsense principle nearby. For example, when my graduate students write thesis defense papers, I always remind them to be sure to engage the arguments against their thesis. A one-sided case is no case at all. But while I agree with that point, it isn't the same thing as your Principle of Total Evidence.

Justin: Okay, I think I've been misunderstood, and it's probably my own fault. I *certainly* don't mean to suggest that we must consider all *possible* information that *anybody, anywhere, and at any time* might have had on the topic before reaching some tentative conclusion. That bar would be way too high for anybody to reach.

So, when I say that people *must consider all the available evidence*, I mean to suggest that they should consider all the evidence that they, themselves, are aware of—the evidence available *to them*.

And, yes, ideally, they will seek out *additional* evidence to consider regardless of whether it confirms their conclusion.

Randal: Okay, that's more plausible (or at least it's less implausible). However, in order for that principle to work you'd still need to define what it means to have evidence available to oneself. After all, every person who is connected to the Internet has access to a staggering degree of information. Must we consult all that information available to us before forming a belief? Am I obliged to corroborate my friend's testimony to London's weather with a comprehensive survey of weather websites? Can't I just take him at his word?

Justin: That's a good point and an interesting question that everybody needs to answer. As modern, privileged persons with access to the Internet, what exactly are our epistemic responsibilities in this regard? I don't know that there is an easy answer here. Obviously I don't think we are obligated to stay on top of *all* the latest research that remotely touches any aspect of our current beliefs. That would be a crazy time-sucker. Yes, it's good to stay informed, but our time is limited, and there are other important things to do and experience in life!

Randal: "Crazy time-sucker"—I like that!

Justin: Glad I could help. Now, with regard to the Principle of Total Evidence, I think we should *at least* consider *all* of those relevant facts whose justificatory reasons we are substantively familiar with.

Randal: Well, if you say so. But this is still vague: I'm not clear on what you would consider to be *substantive familiarity*, so it seems that the question of application remains muddled. I also worry that the principle doesn't require novel *investigation*. It only requires *reflection* on knowledge one already possesses. And this suggests the less thoughtful, aware, and experienced one is, the less one has an obligation to change.

Justin: I've construed the principle to be about what one *should* believe about a claim given the evidence they have. Obviously novel investigations are *also* valuable and one should put a good faith effort toward learning as much as one can (and updating their beliefs accordingly), but that is, I think, a separate issue.

Randal: Perhaps I should get down to brass tacks: if I can reasonably believe it is raining in London simply based on the testimony of a trusted source, as I clearly can, then why can't I reasonably believe God exists based on the testimony of a trusted source?

Justin: Hmm. Allow me answer that in a couple different ways.

Randal: Very well, you are allowed.

Justin: If I'm being asked whether or not testimony is *sufficient* for the-istic belief then, obviously, my answer is that it will depend on the person. Not everybody will have access to the same information, and, as a result, some may rationally disagree about where the total available evidence points *even after* taking on board the additional evidence of testimony. For example, for the person who identifies as an agnostic, testimony about God's existence *may* be sufficient to finally tip the scales toward theistic belief.

Randal: At which point the angels in heaven will rejoice!

Justin: Hold off on sounding the heavenly trumpets. After all, what about an extremely confident atheist, who is only aware of the arguments against God? For *that* person, learning this new evidence about tes-timony will, at best, raise his view of the probability of God only slightly. Clearly then, he would still be a long way from rationally believing that God exists, given the total evidence available to him.

Another interpretation is that you are asking if testimony can, in principle, constitute *some* evidence in support of the conclusion that God exists. If that is your question, then my answer is yes.

Randal: If I hear you right, you agree with me that a person *can* gain a rational belief that God exists through testimony, just like a person can gain a rational belief that it is raining in London through testimony.

Justin: Yeah, so it all depends on the circumstances. If somebody is not terribly confident in their atheism, then, yes, even relatively weak evidence could bring them to theistic belief.

Randal: Okay, great! Now we're getting somewhere!

So just to be clear, you agree that rational belief in God can come about through testimony?

Justin: You've compared the value of testimony for the question of God's existence and the value of testimony for the question of whether it is raining in London.

In the case of hearing from a trusted friend over the phone that it is currently raining in London, I agree that it seems perfectly fine to take that claim at face value if that's the only information you've got. After all, it's not a particularly extraordinary claim. Mundane claims like that only rarely require more information.

But, what if we were to add to the story and say that you also are in London but the sky is clear? Well, it would seem then that your observations of a beautiful, cloudless London sky during that phone call must also be counted among the relevant evidence and factored into your conclusion.

If I were in that situation, I'd be, to say the least, *highly* skeptical. I've experienced rain before, so I know what it feels, smells, and looks like. I also know the conditions under which it usually occurs. Because of that background evidence, I'm likely to think my friend is under some misapprehension when they give their weather report. Of course, there is always the possibility that we'll soon be having a laugh upon realizing we are in entirely different cities named London!

Randal: Oh, you meant London, *England?*! And here I was thinking London, *Ontario!*

Justin: But, I agree with you that, in most cases, these rather ordinary claims are reasonable to believe without any powerful contrary evidence.

Randal: Of course, I agree that our acceptance of testimony is provisional. It is always possible that new evidence can arise that could be sufficient to undermine it. But, if I understand you correctly, that means that you do concede that a person can in principle rationally accept belief in God based on the testimony of others *just so long as they are not aware of any strong evidence to the contrary.* In that sense, testimonial belief in God is very much like any other belief gleaned from testimony.

So then the question is this: are there any people who do believe in God in this manner? And I suspect there are many.

FAITH IN THE EXTRAORDINARY

Justin: Well, let's not get ahead of ourselves here. Of course I agree that it is possible *in principle* for somebody to move rationally toward a theistic position by taking on board evidence that supports theism, just as I agree that it is possible for anybody to move to some position by way of additional evidence so long as the observation actually counts toward the claim.

But, for anybody who doesn't *already* believe in God, the claim "God exists" is likely be an extraordinary claim. Mere testimony, if it is to count as evidence at all, is unlikely to be anything other than very *weak* evidence. That said, if I'm wrong and there is a good argument from religious testimony, I'd be interested in hearing it.

Randal: You say that the claim that God exists will seem extraordinary to those who don't accept it. But that unqualified statement is just not true. Whether it seems extraordinary will surely depend on the person. Certainly, *some* people who are nontheists will find that claim extraordinary. However, others will find it plausible, even if they are not compelled by it. (To borrow William James's famous phrase, they will count it a *live option* for belief.) Nontheists of that sort, who are open to God's existence and who hear persuasive testimony to God's existence from a trusted authority, could be rational in becoming theists based on that testimony.

Justin: That's certainly true. That's why I said that persons who don't already believe in God are *likely* to find it an extraordinary claim. But people who think the evidence is ambiguous or close to ambiguous would be an exception here. These persons could be moved to theism even by relatively weak evidence.

Randal: Here I go nitpicking again, but I just can't help myself. You've talked here about what seems *likely* to you. But it seems to me that you can only say what is likely here if you know the approximate ratio of those who find this belief extraordinary as opposed to those who don't.

Justin: I think that, of the total possible positions that one could have about their atheism, most will think theism extraordinary, at least in the sense that I'm using it.

Randal: I dunno, Justin. That seems like nothing more than a speculative opinion. I'm not sure I can accept that based on your testimony.

The fact is that we can come to believe things that are otherwise extraordinary based on testimony *if we accept the authority of the testifier on that topic.* For example, at first blush it is extraordinary for Mr. and Mrs. Smith to accept the claim that their oak kitchen table consists largely of vibrating packets of energy and empty space. And yet, when their son the physicist comes home for Christmas dinner and informs them that this is indeed the composition of their kitchen table, they could reasonably believe it based on the faith they have in their son and his knowledge and competency about such matters.

Needless to say, this point obviously isn't limited to the composition of oak tables. In other words, you can't preclude the possibility that some people could have an equivalent status as witnesses such that their testimony could be sufficient to overcome the prima facie incredulity that an atheist might otherwise have to the claim that God exists.

Justin: Well, allow me to interject here to make what I think is an important point.

Randal: What if I say no?

Justin: The Sherpa commands it.

Randal: So first you scold me for overdoing the Sherpa bit and now *you're* going to play the Sherpa card? That's merciless.

Justin: Now, I want to be clear in that I agree that Mr. and Mrs. Smith are rational to accept their son's testimony, even though it initially seemed extraordinary to them given the *commonsense* background knowledge they had to work with.

One of the reasons they would be rational to accept their son's testimony about what would otherwise seem to be an extraordinary claim, is that they have a background or preexisting trust in the reliability of an institution of learning from which their son has acquired a degree, its vetting capabilities, and the broader body of scientific knowledge that is serving as its source.

To see my point, imagine that Mr. and Mrs. Smith were atheists and their son comes home from seminary to visit with the family. Over dinner, he starts telling them about the Holy Trinity. In this scenario, they are unlikely to be moved because they place no trust in the claims, methodologies, or traditions of the seminary their son is attending.

Both stories have the parents hearing an extraordinary claim from their son. And yet their reactions differ because of the origin of that claim.

Randal: Great, so then if Mr. and Mrs. Smith are Christians who have a preexisting trust in the reliability of the institution of the *church*, you're okay with them accepting their seminarian son's testimony to the Trinity?

Justin: Yes. If Mr. and Mrs. Smith are *already* Christians, I suppose I'm fine with them being Trinitarian Christians, so long as they can defend the coherence of the doctrine.

Randal: Hey, we're definitely making some good progress here. However, I will say your added requirement that they must be able to defend the coherence of the Trinity seems rather unfair since they presumably don't need to defend the coherence of quantum physics to accept their son's testimony in the science scenario.

That point aside, you've agreed that people can come to have rational beliefs about God through testimony, potentially including rich doctrines like the Trinity. Having gotten that far, let me up the ante here a bit. If we accept the standard philosophical definition of knowledge as "justified true belief," then it follows that, if God does indeed exist, the person who accepts that belief based on the trusted testimony of another person could also *know* that God exists based on that testimony. *Right?*

Justin: With most claims, even those that seem profoundly implausible given *our* current beliefs about the world, it's quite easy to *imagine* epistemic situations in which the relevant evidence available to some *other* individual was such that it would be rational for her to accept them as true.

Randal: As in . . . ?

Justin: Imagine a child perceives, as most do, their parents as testimonial authorities. In such a context, testimony from her parents about a magical Santa Claus could be rationally met with her assenting to belief in the gift-bearing man in a red suit capable of freezing time on Christmas Eve.

Randal: Ahh, a common misunderstanding. You see, Santa doesn't actually *freeze* time. He just moves *really fast*, kind of like the Flash. Other than that, I'm tracking with you. Can you give another illustration?

Justin: Imagine a curious child who has surveyed arguments for and against garden fairies and has, as a result of his investigation, concluded that the *total* evidence of which he is aware fails to discriminate between fairyism and afairyism. He might then call himself an agnostic about fairies. In this context, too, even relatively weak additional evidence could kindly escort a middle-of-the-epistemic-road agnostic to a fairyist position once taken aboard.

Randal: Okay, I have to ask. Are you aware of any fairy arguments that might tip the balance?

Justin: Don't worry, I'm not aware of any such arguments. I'm simply drawing out a hypothetical comparison. Admittedly, it's a bit fantastical.

Randal: For you maybe, but not for the five-year-old devotee of Tinker Bell!

Justin: Haha, true enough. The fact is that, given that most unbelievers (about God) *do* know about the variety and conflicting nature of testimony regarding supernatural entities in general and God in particular, most have good reason to not grant mere testimony very much weight—if any at all. For not only is massive theological testimonial disagreement—disagreement among believers about theological concepts—and their associated testimony wildly surprising on theism, it also gives us reason at least to look closer at the source and motivation behind the testimony rather than just factor it in unquestioningly. Perhaps the one giving the testimony is just repeating the words of a rather credulous individual.

Being on the tail end of a game of testimony telephone is rarely a safe place to be.

Randal: I agree that many unbelievers will be aware of evidence that they believe is sufficient to undermine testimony for God's existence. For example, Jim the atheist returns home for Thanksgiving. As the family sits down for their turkey, his grandmother says, "Jim, I know that my redeemer liveth. He's real, Jim!" That testimony probably won't be enough to overcome Jim's disbelief.

Justin: Right. Unfortunately, the fact that an atheist is unlikely to be moved by bold assertions of God's existence from close family members hardly ever renders such familial assertions less frequent. This holds especially true during holidays!

Randal: But, even so, my point is that there is nothing wrong in principle with Jim encountering testimonial evidence of sufficient strength to overwhelm his objections. Imagine, for example, that Jim's father, a world-famous atheist philosopher, follows up grandmother's testimony like this: "Jim, I agree with your grandmother. I just had an extraordinary experience with the living God that has transformed my perspective. I'm not an atheist anymore!" His father then goes on to relay an amazing personal experience that changed him from being an atheist to being a theist.

I don't know whether Jim's father's testimony would be sufficient to change Jim's mind. Certainly we wouldn't expect it to do so overnight. After all, people don't typically change their worldviews quickly. But even so, his father's testimony clearly has *some* weight, and, from an evidential perspective, it is stronger than that of his grandmother. Given all this, I think you need to be open to the extent to which testimony based on things like an individual's personal experience or their evaluation of evidence can be a catalyst for others acquiring the rational belief that God exists.

Justin: I don't believe that I've said anything suggesting otherwise. Of course, different qualities or contexts of different testimonial assertions will likely differ in strength.

Randal: I am heartened to say that I think we really have made progress here. To summarize, it is possible that people can rationally come to believe God exists, and to accept a range of doctrinal claims about God, all based on the testimony of others. Moreover, if those doctrines are true, then a person could potentially come to *know* them through testimony.

I would also add that all that you've said about atheists being reluctant to accept Christian testimony applies equally to Christians being reluctant to accept atheist testimony. So that definitely cuts both ways.

Justin: I think it's important to note that I've consistently maintained that, if testimony is to count as evidence for God at all, then, for most of those without belief in God, mere testimony will not suffice to bring them to rational belief in God. Nothing I've said here should be interpreted as anything remotely resembling a lack of openness *to* or an in-principle dismissal *of* the ability of testimony, in some specific circumstances, to rationally bring about belief in God.

Randal: We agree on that.

Justin: But perhaps that's enough testimony talk for now.

Randal: We agree on that too. Or perhaps I should say *I accept that testimony!* (Ha ha! I crack me up!)

Justin: Oh, brother.

Randal: Anyway, I vote for a topic change. Any ideas?

Chapter 3

THE PROBLEM OF MASSIVE THEOLOGICAL DISAGREEMENT

Justin: Well, remember my claim about massive theological disagreement? Now is as good a time as any to unpack my thinking on this.

Randal: That sounds like a fine idea. It builds nicely on our faith and rationality conversation. And, even better, now I get to criticize one of your arguments!

Justin: Go easy on me, will you?

Randal: Not likely, pal.

WHAT IS EVIDENCE?

Justin: Now, before we go diving headfirst into that argument in particular, it might be worth getting clearer on the concept of evidence more generally.

Randal: Excellent suggestion. That's another one of those words we use all the time, like *God* and *faith*, but we rarely stop to explain or define it. The floor is yours.

Justin: Philosopher of science Colin Howson writes, "To say that a body of information is evidence in favor of a hypothesis is to say that the hypothesis receives some degree of support or confirmation from that information."[1]

Randal: Good definition. So how does that work in our conversation?

Justin: Well, in our conversation about God, it means that evidence favoring God will be observations that we should expect to observe if God exists but *less* so if God does not exist. If we come across new-to-us observations that fit that description, we should adjust the probability we currently place on God upward. Particularly strong evidence for God would be observations that are very likely on the assumption that God exists but very unlikely on the assumption that

65

God does not exist. Strong evidence requires more of a shift in our probability estimates about God than does weaker evidence.

Randal: Makes sense.

Justin: Moreover, for us to talk about evidence in a conversation about God, we need to be able to be in a position to say something about what God is likely or unlikely to create, allow to happen, or prevent outright. We must be able to say that, if God exists, X is likely to be observed and Y is unlikely to be observed. This is an important point to which we will almost certainly return.

For now, allow me to give a nontheological example of how this might work.

Randal: Hmmm, okay I'll allow the example, but only because I'm in a good mood.

Justin: Mark becomes hungry for a snack, only to realize that the chocolate chip cookies he bought from the store have gone missing. He looks around and can't seem to find any sign of them. Mark then considers the possibility that Seth, his four-year-old son, ate them.

Randal: Ahh, yes, I bet Seth did it. The Cookie Monster T-shirt is a dead giveaway.

Justin: This hypothesis seems plausible enough—it's not unlikely on his current information. After all, Mark is aware that Seth has a bit of a sweet tooth. But he also knows that Seth can be a sloppy eater, so when Seth returns from playing in the yard, and Mark notices cookie crumbs on Seth's clothing, those cookie crumbs count as strong evidence in favor of Seth's guilt here for at least two important reasons. The first reason is that observing crumbs on Seth's clothing would be very surprising if Seth did *not* take the cookies. The second is that observing cookie crumbs on Seth's clothing *would* be expected if Seth *did* take the cookies and, well, gave into his cookie fandom.

Randal: And don't forget that Cookie Monster T-shirt.

Justin: Hah, yes. There's that, too. How could I forget?

Randal: But anyway, keep going. Now that we've got a sense of the meaning of evidence, perhaps you can draw a picture to set up your argument.

Justin: That sounds fair.

Consider then, Tom and Mike—new neighbors living within the same apartment building—sorry, there are no snacks to be found in this story. For business reasons they're told, the landlord only communicates privately with each tenant. However, the tenants communicate casually with each other on occasion and, as a result, they've discovered some big incompatibilities in their beliefs about the landlord.

Randal: Like what?

Justin: Well, for example, Tom says the landlord wants all residents to pay rent by check. Mike insists that the landlord commands all residents pay their rent in cash. Tom says the landlord is a woman, but Mike insists the landlord is a man.

Randal: Okay, this is starting to get weird.

Justin: Right, and that's exactly the point: it's unexpected.

In addition to *that* weirdness, Tom claims that the landlord assures him that all residents pay $700 for their rent, and Mike says that the landlord only demands $500 from all. These disagreements—some important and some admittedly trivial—would understandably create a tension between new neighbors as well as between them and their landlord. Such disagreements will assuredly have a negative effect on the residents forming good relationships with their landlord.

Randal: Wow, that certainly would be a strange situation. I'm guessing Tom would be especially miffed because he's paying $200 a month more than Mike.

Justin: I know I would! This kind of disagreement between persons convinced of their own experiences is ripe for an escalation of conflict with even the best and most genuine of intentions. At the very least, it's going to negatively affect the relationship they have with their landlord, as it will raise all sorts of suspicions.

Moreover, it suggests a number of flaws in the landlord and his/her business practices. After all, a fair and efficient landlord (if there be such a thing) has many reasons *not* to allow such confusion to persist in and about his/her place of business and would intervene to correct discrepancies or misinterpretations of his/her words and policies. And yet there are no reasons for the landlord *not* to intervene and correct misunderstandings. These hostilities are antithetical to the fulfillment of the basic goals of a landlord. As it stands then, for Mark and Tom, their perpetual disagreements and confusion are evidence against their landlord being both efficient and fair.

Randal: I'll agree with you on that. Although I'll add that in this scenario at least part of the problem could be *competency*. That landlord could be well intentioned but simply incompetent for the task.

Justin: Yes, it could be an issue of competency, but, presumably, competency is assumed within the definition of a *fair and efficient* landlord.

Randal: True enough.

Justin: Anyway, I want to suggest that a parallel argument can be made here with respect to disagreements and confusion about claims of considerably greater importance to theists.

Randal: Darn, I was hoping we could keep talking about the Mark and Tom story. Landlord and tenant law is one of my burning passions.

Justin: You must never have rented. The kinds of disagreements I'm wanting to bring an argumentative light to are disagreements over how one might become morally reconciled to God, what God is like, or what God wants us to do. Which of the revered ancient texts, if any, has God authored or inspired? These questions are central to the lives of most theists. However, these same questions are subjects of wide disagreement and confusion among theists. Disagreements like these can and often do lead to profound acts of violence between individuals and populations.

DOES RELIGION LEAD TO VIOLENCE?

Randal: Sorry, but I need to interject.

Justin: See what I mean? You've just inflicted a profound act of religious violence on my word flow, zealot!

Randal: Yeah, I apologize for my fanatical barbarism. But I still need to challenge the assumption that religious disagreements often, as you put it, "lead to profound acts of violence between individuals and populations." That's a popular idea in the skeptic and new atheist literature, but I don't believe it is accurate.

Justin: Well, you'll have to forgive me for raising a particularly skeptical brow here. What you've just said seems like a claim more easily asserted than supported. What is your thought process here?

Randal: Not going to accept my testimony, eh? Well, I'll see your skeptical eyebrow and raise you a double brow of quizzical incredulity.

Nothing captures the perceived link between religion and violence more starkly than 9/11, a horrific terrorist act in which the terrorists all held to a form of radical Islam. This event was so shocking that it provided the catalyst for new atheists like Sam Harris to take up their rhetorical arms against the religious foe.

So let's consider the phenomenon of suicide terrorism, a type of act that constitutes for many the purest and most disturbing expression of the link between violence and religious dogma. In his 2005 book *Dying to Win: The Strategic Logic of Suicide Terrorism*, political scientist Robert Pape investigates every act of suicide terrorism from 1980 to 2003. And Pape concludes, "The data show that there is little connection between suicide terrorism and Islamic fundamentalism, *or any one of the world's religions.* In fact, the leading instigators of suicide attacks are the Tamil Tigers in Sri Lanka, a Marxist-Leninist group whose members are from Hindu families but who are *adamantly opposed to religion.*"[2]

Justin: That's pretty interesting.

Randal: Right. And it invites the obvious question: if most suicide terrorists are not driven by religion, then what is it that motivates them? Pape observes that almost all acts of suicide terrorism are motivated by a geopolitical goal, namely "to compel modern democracies to withdraw military forces from territory that the terrorists consider to be their homeland."[3] While Pape recognizes that religion may serve as one tool of this nationalistic drive to expel the foreigner, it is "rarely the root cause."

Justin: Well, okay, but it's certainly no secret that violence is a much broader category than the particularly modern form caused by suicide terrorism. Just because religious disagreement may not be the primary cause or rationale for one form of particularly modern violence, that alone does not render false the claim that religious disagreements can and do often lead or contribute to violence between individuals and populations.

Randal: Fair enough. However, I would add that the type of violence represented by contemporary suicide terrorists has ancient antecedents. Consider, for example, the story of Samson's suicide in Judges 16:23–30 in which he destroys a temple filled with civilians.

Justin: Fair point. I should also say that my claim is perfectly compatible with the related and obviously true claim that there are other factors (nationalistic, political, etc.) that can and often do contribute to violence in important ways. But let me be clear in that I certainly agree with you that, in general, claims tying religion to violence are particularly susceptible to exaggeration and oversimplification from persons with an axe to grind against religion, but I don't believe I've made that mistake here.

Randal: At the very least, I'd advise caution against simply labelling a particular instance of violence as religious to the exclusion of a myriad of geopolitical, cultural, social, and economic factors. On this point, the new atheists have cast a lot of heat, if not a lot of light, with their grossly reductive analysis of events like 9/11 as being generated solely or primarily by religion. Generally there is a multiplicity of factors that lead people to participate in this kind of violence.

Having said that, might I add that the same goes when religious folk try to draw simple associations between atheism or secularism and some negative social effects. Either way, axe grinding fits rather poorly with generous and nuanced dialogue!

Justin: Amen to that, you violent word-flow-interrupting extremist.

Randal: Christians united can never be defeated! Christians united can never be defeated! Woot woot!

But perhaps that's enough cheering for now. Where were we?

DISAGREEMENT ABOUT LANDLORDS, PARENTS, AND GOD

Justin: The purpose of my tale of two tenants is that, just as the perpetual disagreement between tenants on certain questions counts as evidence against a fair and efficient landlord, massive theological disagreement between theists on certain questions counts as evidence against God.

It seems quite clear to me that a perfectly loving God, in seeking relationships with those willing and eager for relationships with the divine, would prevent profound theological disagreements and confusion to persist among his loved ones—especially to the point of violence. Given how surprising this widespread theological disagreement is on theism and how entirely unsurprising, expected even, it would be on an atheistic hypothesis, it should count as strong evidence against theism.

Do you agree?

Randal: First off, I love the title "The Tale of Two Tenants." It sounds like a story from *Grimm's Fairy Tales*!

Justin: Like the Bible! Did you hear that rim shot?

Randal: Whoa, that's a low blow.

But while the title is great, it seems to me that your analogy doesn't quite accomplish what you want. After all, disagreement between Mark and Tom does *not* provide evidence for either one of them to doubt the *existence* of the landlord. As you note, at best it provides reason for them to doubt some aspect of the landlord's character or competence.

Justin: Right, it would be pretty silly for them to doubt the very existence of the landlord outright. The purpose of my story was in arguing that such disagreement provides evidence against a *fair and efficient* landlord *specifically*. In the parallel case of God, it counts as evidence against the existence of God as we've specifically defined her earlier in our conversation, as all-powerful, all-knowing, and morally perfect.

Randal: That's a good point.

Justin: Thank you. Well, this has been a nice chat, Randal. However, I've got a train to catch.

Randal: Hold up there, grasshopper. It's still not clear to me that this scenario would provide grounds to doubt the existence of an all-powerful, all-knowing, morally perfect God.

Justin: Whaaaat?

Randal: Consider Tom's epistemic situation for a moment. Based on his experience, he is firmly convinced that the landlord is, in fact, a woman, and that the landlady wants the payments made by check. When Tom then hears Mark insisting that the landlord is a man who demands cash payments, Tom could conclude many things. He might think, for example, that Mark is simply mistaken or confused. Or he might suspect that Mark is lying. Or it could be that the landlady has ambiguous gender characteristics, which he misinterpreted, and that the landlady gave special instructions to Mark to pay by cash given his poor credit history. There are many possibilities Tom might consider before he rejects his beliefs about the landlady's gender or that she has requested payments by check.

Similarly, when two people report having different experiences of God and different beliefs about God, there are all sorts of explanations one might consider to explain the divergence (e.g., personal error, divine accommodation) before concluding that no God exists at all.

Justin: Okay, okay. I'm afraid I haven't been as clear as I could have. I am not making the general argument that any disagreement between two persons about some matter should lead them to doubt their respective convictions. There are situations in which it is possible for them to continue in their disagreement in a rational way.

Randal: I'm glad to hear that. So then can you unpack your critique of theism a bit more? Things are still a bit blurry.

Justin: Well, the point is that the disagreement *itself* counts against the hypothesis of a fair and efficient landlord and that this is relevantly similar to the problem with massive theological disagreement.

That said, perhaps a better analogy for my argument can be found in a parent/child relationship. Let's now say that Mark and Tom are young children, brothers even, being raised by a single parent. Let's also say that they have key disagreements about how their parent wants them to act and how best to have a relationship with their parent. Unsurprisingly, these disagreements on important details lead to some tension and even the occasional fight between the children. Each child is as certain that they are right as they are that the other is dead wrong. These disagreements, and the conflicts birthed from them, could be easily prevented by their parent simply clarifying the point of contention and notifying them both of who is right and who is wrong so that nothing stands in the way of relationship between the children and their mother. But, unlike a normal, loving parent, this parent remains utterly silent. The parent allows sizeable disagreements and deep confusions about important relational matters to persist and even boil over into violence occasionally.

Randal: I see. A "hands-off" parent, eh?

Justin: Arguably, a neglectful parent. A parent who perhaps has no business being a parent.

Randal: Uh oh, I see where this is going!

Justin: The question I'm interested in is whether or not this disagreement and confusion among the children counts as evidence for them against the idea that their parent is loving. Of course, in the case of God—who is defined as essentially morally perfect—we are questioning God's very existence, rather than just her moral character.

Randal: Once again, I find it important to point out that one must be very careful about drawing overly facile connections between religious disagreement and violence or conflict. In your familial analogy you refer to two siblings who disagree about their parent's instructions, a disagreement that in turn gives rise to conflicts between the two siblings.

But rarely are matters this simple.

Justin: Fair enough.

Randal: I often find myself disagreeing with others over various matters (as we are doing right now). But mere disagreement is not, in itself, warrant for conflict, let alone violence. Consequently, if two siblings (or any other two individuals) do get into a conflict that descends into mistrust, anger, and perhaps even violence, it doesn't follow that the initial disagreement *caused* the conflict. Perhaps those in disagreement resorted to conflict because of other, preexisting factors. It could be, for example, that each individual already harbored a brooding hostility toward the other, and this disagreement merely provided the occasion for those hostilities to become visible.

Justin: Point taken. I'm simply pointing to the fact that disagreement, and the certainty often associated with metaphysical disagreement in particular, can *contribute* to these tensions.

Randal: With that in mind, let's consider again our siblings, Mark and Tom. Occasionally they find themselves at odds over what their parent has commanded or requested. Disagreement like this could lead to all sorts of outcomes, including puzzlement, doubt, and a more thoughtful reflection on one's evidence for their own view. Conflict, such as that which gives rise to physical altercations, is only one possible outcome.

Justin: Yes, but I fail to see how this undermines the argument in a significant way. It's not merely an argument about disagreements that lead to fights.

Randal: The point is that if Mark and Tom respond to disagreement with *fisticuffs* rather than friendly reflection and dialogue, we must ask what it is about Mark and Tom as persons and their relationship that leads to this particularly violent outcome. In short, a significant degree of culpability for the conflict must rest on *their* shoulders. You can't attribute it all to the parent.

Justin: Perhaps that's true with regard to *some* of their fights but certainly not all. Some may genuinely be partially the result of clashing and equally certain convictions about what they should be doing or who knows their parent best.

Randal: Sure, but the higher our initial estimation of the parent's fitness, the less likely we would be to conclude the parent was inept in allowing the conflict.

Justin: That's true. However, I've never claimed that the children should conclude their parent is a poor parent on this one piece of evidence. The conclusion here was simply that their disagreement provides them *some* evidence for that conclusion or that the disagreement supports the idea of a poor parent over a loving parent.

Randal: Okay, well, we can enrich the story a bit more. Imagine that the parent was aware of the poor, festering relationship between Mark and Tom, and so that parent purposefully allowed disagreement to arise precisely to provide a catalyst for conflict.

Now you might be wondering: why would a parent do that? Obviously a good parent wouldn't seek to instigate conflict as an end in itself. But a good parent certainly *could* allow conflict to arise in order to reveal the deep, ongoing problems in the relationship between Mark and Tom, so that these problems might finally be dealt with. The conflict could be painful but also therapeutic, like lancing a boil.

Justin: I don't know of any decent parent who would allow their children to come to blows over a disagreement, simply so that they could all sit down and reflect on the situation afterward, like the ending of some half-hour sitcom. A parent who implants disagreement and then knowingly does nothing to prevent the violence that flows from it should be reported to Child Protective Services.

Randal: Wow, strong words.

Justin: More importantly, violence arising from differences in religious beliefs—as with most other conflicts—hardly ever ends in anything other than further zealous confidence in their respective religious beliefs.

Oh, and sometimes a body count.

Randal: A body count?!

Is it just me or is the rhetoric starting to get a bit heated in here?

Justin: Well, you're an open-minded religious person who finds the benefit in calm discourse. Not everybody is this way. Fervent zealotry does exist, and sometimes it can be expressed in damaging ways.

Randal: Amen to that! I appreciate your brave takedown of the new atheists!

Justin: Oh, I see what you did there.

Randal: My point is that a good parent could purposefully allow some degree of disagreement among his/her children for the ultimate good of the children. And until we know this *isn't* the case, the mere existence of disagreement and resulting conflict is not in itself a reason to question the goodness or capability of the parent.

Nor is the kind of scenario I've described implausible or contrived. Indeed, I think parents *often* do things like this. Based on their knowledge of their children and their desire to ensure that their children grow and develop in their character, parents may allow states of affairs to exist that might appear to the casual observer to be inept or improper. But one should simply withhold such judgments until one has a better grasp of the background of the situation and the intentions of the parent, and all the more so if one believes at the outset that the parent is knowledgeable and wise.

Needless to say, if caution is recommended in judging a mere human's parenting skills, how much more is caution warranted when considering the skills of an infinitely good, wise, and powerful being?

Justin: Okay, but remember my argument doesn't claim that a parent or God would prevent any and all disagreement. I'm particularly interested in disagreements on important relational and moral matters.

In the parent/child analogy, a parent would prevent disagreement on important issues like how the children should behave, what their parent wants from them, or how best to have a relationship with their parent. This is compatible with the parents also allowing a large array of disagreement in other aspects of their child's life.

In the case of theism, God might understandably allow deep disagreement over various trivial things. But when it comes to questions of what view of God is correct, what God wishes for us, and how to enter relationship and/or reconcile with God, that's another thing entirely. And so, this too is compatible with allowing a large array of disagreement in every other area of life.

Randal: I see what you're saying. However, it seems arbitrary to concede my general point but then insist that there is this *one* area where a parent would *never* allow disagreement among their children.

Justin: I think the distinction is justified by the fact that these more important disagreements have negative effects on both the relationship with the parent and each child's perception of the other's relationship with the parent. It breeds jealousy and conflicting certainty. Moreover, it's so easily resolved.

Randal: Negative consequences certainly *could* occur in a case like this. But I don't think you've given a good reason to believe such negative consequences are an inevitability in this kind of disagreement.

THE ARGUMENT FROM MASSIVE THEOLOGICAL DISAGREEMENT (MTD)

Justin: It might be helpful if I was a bit more explicit in my presentation of the argument. As I've said earlier, this argument is an attempt to provide evidence against the existence of God. It might be valuable then to get a bit more explicit in how the argument is supposed to work. So, what exactly do I mean by the observation of *massive theological disagreement* (MTD)?

Randal: You took the words right out of my mouth! What *do* you mean?

Justin: I suppose great minds think alike.

Randal: Or it could just be that Caucasian North American males think alike.

Justin: That too.

Well, first of all, we are talking about theological disagreement among those who believe that God, as we've defined here, does in fact exist. There are many such persons in the actual world—most of which identify with one of the three Western religious traditions.

Secondly, we aren't talking about just any theological disagreement. Some theological disagreements are relatively trivial when compared to the kinds of disagreement I want to bring attention to. The theological disagreements I'm after are those dealing with key issues, such as the nature of God, her revelation to us, how we are supposed to live, and how best to enter into/maintain a meaningful relationship with God.

Randal: Right-o, a lot of good things there. But can you pull this all together into an argument?

Justin: I sure hope so. The argument I'm attempting to unpack seems simple enough. It consists of a mere two premises and a conclusion.

Randal: Short and sweet; I like it.

Justin: The *first premise* states that, on the denial of theism, MTD is likely to be true. On the denial of theism, humans were not created by an omnipotent, omniscient, and perfectly moral being. Therefore, if beliefs in such a being still arise in such an atheistic world, then they are not the result of God making herself available for personal relationship. If there exists no God and therefore no profound religious truth toward which a God could properly guide willing persons, then we would expect a variety of contradictory religious traditions to bubble up by way of the variety in personalities, cultures, etc.

Randal: I'll grant you that this is a plausible scenario, at least at first blush.

Justin: The *second premise* is that, on the truth of theism, MTD is unlikely to be true. On theism, our expectations unfold in a profoundly different way. If God exists, she would want every one of her willing and open creatures to have the truth about her nature, revelation, and how they can best live. Only then will they be able to live out the purpose for which they were created. Anyone who believed in and submitted to her willingly would then have this information provided to them.

Contrary to the religiously divided world we see, theism gives us strong reason to expect a single world religion or set of doctrines— at least with respect to the most important issues.

Randal: Got it. I can certainly see why *you* believe God would secure religious agreement.

Justin: Now that I've stated the two premises, I should probably show what conclusion follows from them. To do that, I have to introduce something called the Likelihood Principle. Elliott Sober writes, "Observation O supports hypothesis H1 more than it supports H2 if and only if the probability of the observation on H1 is greater than the probability of the observation on H2."[4]

Randal: Sounds technical. Perhaps I could apply the Likelihood Principle to a practical example to make sure we're on the same page.

Justin: Yeah, that might be helpful.

Randal: So let's say the observation is "The pavement is wet," hypothesis H1 is "It's raining," while H2 is "It isn't raining." All things being equal, the observation better accords with H1 than H2. Is that what you're thinking?

Justin: Yes, that's exactly right. The observation better fits H1 because a hypothesis that states that it is raining would make wet pavement likely, while a hypothesis like H2 does nothing by way of predicting wet pavement.

Notice this is true even if the defender of H2 asserts additional claims in an effort to make the wet pavement consistent with or less surprising on H2. For example, the defender of H2 could assert that, even though it wasn't raining, a nearby fire hydrant had recently sprayed water all over the pavement. However, unless we have good, independent reasons for thinking that such an event occurred (like signs that someone has tampered with the hydrant), the additional claim does little to undermine the inductive inference at work.

Now that we have a better grasp of how the Likelihood Principle functions, we can plug in the information from the first two premises defended above. When we do that, we get the following conclusion:

The fact of MTD supports atheism more than it supports theism.

Now we can put the pieces together to see how the argument works:

Premise one: On the denial of theism, the observation MTD is likely.

Premise two: On the affirmation of theism, the observation MTD is unlikely (or less likely).

Conclusion (by way of LP): The fact of MTD supports atheism more than it supports theism.

Okay, now that I've presented the basic argument and some of the reasons in support of it, I want to hand it over to you, Randal. Perhaps we can start with the first premise? I take it you have some comments.

DEBATING PREMISE ONE

Randal: Excellent. So let's go back to your assertion that if there is *no* God then we should expect, as you said, "contradictory religious traditions to bubble up by way of the variety in personalities, cultures, etc." And if there *is* a God then we should expect "a single world religion or set of doctrines—at least with respect to the most important issues."

Justin: Yes, I think that's what we should expect given those two hypotheses.

Randal: And I'm thinking to myself, who is this *we* of which you speak? It sure doesn't include me.

Justin: Oh?

Randal: So I'm going to aim to reply with an undercutting defeater. For our readers who may not be familiar with the concept, a defeater is a line of evidence against a particular claim. There are two types of defeater. A *rebutting defeater* seeks to show that a claim is false while an *undercutting defeater* seeks to undermine our basis for thinking a claim is true.

Justin: That's an important distinction. Perhaps you could unpack it a bit more though.

Randal: Sure, let me give an example of an undercutting defeater. Imagine that Mrs. Jones is found dead in her home after a violent struggle. The crime scene investigators then discover her husband's DNA underneath two fingernails. That discovery would seem to suggest a struggle and thus provide evidence supportive of Mr. Jones's guilt. However, when the detectives confront Mr. Jones with this evidence, Mr. Jones explains that the night before her murder, Mrs. Jones had scraped a fleck of food off her husband's cheek at dinner. This claim is later corroborated by other eyewitnesses. Since this scenario would account for the presence of Mr. Jones's DNA being under Mrs. Jones's fingernails, it undercuts the strength of that evidence. To be clear, it doesn't show Mr. Jones is innocent: it only undermines the basis to think he is guilty. But that point is nonetheless very important. So that's how an undercutting defeater works.

In like manner, if I show that you have failed to demonstrate that MTD is more likely on atheism than theism, I thereby undercut your basis to conclude that MTD is supportive of atheism.

Justin: Okay. I think I follow.

Randal: Good enough for me. So let's take your first claim. If God doesn't exist, it is certainly *possible* that religious diversity could emerge through a variety of personalities, cultures, etc. But I'm going to add that it is *also* possible that without God the force of particular personalities, social conditions, and other variables could result in widespread religious agreement on core issues.

Justin: Okay. So we have identified at least two *possibilities* . . .

Randal: But note that this isn't just wild speculation. There could well be a *logic* to the emergence of this kind of agreement that makes it more likely than not that it will emerge in time. Perhaps, for example, blind selective pressures are more often than not sufficient to weed out substantial religious disagreement in a population, thereby eventually securing commonality in religious belief as the norm. Just as the well-established process of convergent evolution allows for similar biological traits to evolve independently in similar environments (e.g., marsupial and placental animals), so it could be with the evolution of religious ideas.

And that brings us to the pivotal question you need to address: *how much more likely* is it on naturalism that substantial religious disagreement will emerge as opposed to broad religious commonality? I don't see that you have provided any hard evidence to support your claim that religious disagreement really is substantially more likely to emerge on naturalism. And as a result, it seems to me that this leg of your argument rests on little more than your subjective intuitions that it's so.

Justin: Just as a quick note, my statement was that MTD is more to be expected on *atheism* than it is on theism. My argument is a defense of atheism and says nothing about naturalism. That said, the conclusion of the argument is surely consistent with naturalism and the argument could be run that way as well.

Randal: Ack! You're right. Sorry about that. Pardon me while I self-flagellate as punishment.

Justin: No problem. I can wait.

Randal: Ouch! Ouch!

Justin: Okay, now to your objection. You've challenged my justification for premise one by highlighting a possibility. You've argued for the possibility that, on atheism, varied cultures and personalities would *eventually* lead us to theological unity after a period of massive disagreement such as we observe today.

I think that's an interesting approach to the argument, but I'm not without a response.

Randal: Alright, I've braced myself. Fire when ready!

Justin: Okay, well, it should be clear by now that the *evidential* argument from massive theological disagreement makes room for such possibilities. If one wanted to bring up such a thing by itself, it wouldn't be sufficient to undermine the argument. See, we would *also* need to be provided with compelling *independent reasons* for thinking that this is how things are likely to go on atheism.

To your credit, you attempt to fulfill that larger order by suggesting that, possibly, it is some future unnamed *selective pressure* working on populations that may be up to the task of bringing us *from* theological disagreement *to* theological unanimity on atheism.

Randal: I understand that your argument requires you to find it enormously improbable that religious agreement would emerge via undirected selective pressures.

Justin: My argument only requires such emergence of religious agreement to be significantly less probable on atheism than it is on theism.

Randal: Sure, well, your great surprise here doesn't ring true to me. You believe selective pressures had a hand in producing the world's staggering biodiversity, from aardvarks to zebras. And in the midst of that diversity we find extraordinary convergence. To note one example, selective pressures led to the independent evolutionary emergence of eyes more than fifty times. Given that biological diversity and convergence emerge with such regularity, why are you so surprised that selective pressures could also have helped produce something far less amazing, like broad religious agreement in a population?

Justin: I must admit to being a bit confused here. Earth is a big place, and its environments are varied. From grasslands and deserts to forests and oceans, these different environments have dramatically different selective pressures and ecological niches. Those dramatically different selective pressures are one of the main reasons why we should not be surprised at the wide variety of life that exists.

Given the wide variety of environments and selective pressures, your claim that a broad religious monolith is somehow *far less amazing* than the wide variety of life forms is, it seems to me, completely backward.

Your main claim though, is that it's plausible that, at some time in the future, there will emerge a selective pressure that has been largely silent till now that brings about eventual religious agreement even if atheism is true.

I think it's important to point out that, not only have we not been provided even a possible candidate for a selective pressure that is up to the ambitious task of eventual broad religious agreement, we also lack an explanation for *why* such a pressure would plausibly emerge in the future to encourage a unification specifically aimed at metaphysical beliefs about a God that does not even exist!

Randal: And to think I was going to tell you not to pull any punches. Looks like that won't be necessary!

Justin: Your proposal amounts to little more than an imaginative and ad hoc *"what if?"* scenario. Nearly everything we know about how humans react in the face of disagreement generally (and metaphysical disagreement in particular) leads us to expect individuals to dig in their heels when confronted with contrary views that challenge their own beliefs.

Randal: Okay, now that you've said your piece, I need to make two points here.

First, we need to be crystal clear on your argument. Your premise isn't merely an assertion about belief formation in the actual world. Rather, it ranges across all possible worlds that contain rational agents that could form religious beliefs. With that in mind, I take your claim to be that, granting the truth of atheism, it follows that across that infinite number of possible worlds, the set of worlds in which large numbers of individuals attain religious agreement is substantially smaller than the set in which they do not. This claim is then taken as support for the conclusion that the MTD in the actual world is less surprising on atheism than on theism.

But if you want to *defend* that premise, you can't limit yourself to the actual world (i.e., the universe that in fact exists). That is, it isn't enough to challenge me to present specific selective pressures or psychological mechanisms that could naturally cultivate religious agreement in the actual world. Rather, the onus is on *you* to demonstrate that across the range of possible worlds (that is, the various possible ways things could have been) with individuals who hold religious beliefs, that comparatively few of those worlds will have mechanisms that will be likely to create that religious agreement naturally, that is, apart from divine intervention.

Justin: Right. So, this is where background knowledge (or background evidence) becomes relevant. While it hasn't yet been stated explicitly, my argument has been operating under the much more limited set of worlds where human beings exist and have come to exist by the selective pressures at work in the actual world.

Randal: My point still stands, since that subset of possible worlds is still unimaginably vast.

Second, when it comes to the actual world, I deny your claim that I've offered nothing more than an "imaginative '*what if.*'" There are well-known psychological mechanisms that explain how large numbers of human beings come into agreement on particular topics ranging from food to culture to philosophy to religion.

To note one example, consider the bandwagon effect. This is a very well-studied phenomenon according to which rates of individual adoption of particular beliefs or practices accelerate in proportion to the growing numbers of those who have already adopted the belief or practice. This positive-feedback effect could explain how religious agreement emerges naturally in a world like ours, to say nothing of that infinite number of other possible worlds, with heretofore unimagined psychological mechanisms and selective pressures.

Justin: I think it is vitally important to realize that the bandwagon effect doesn't work in isolation. There are other psychological tendencies at work in human decision-making. It's just not probable that the bandwagon effect would somehow magically begin to override everything else and bring us toward global theological agreement on atheism.

EVALUATING PREMISE TWO

Randal: Yeah, well I never suggested the bandwagon effect would *magically override everything else*. I offer it simply as one part of a very plausible account of how we might expect religious agreement to emerge naturally, wholly apart from divine intervention.

Anyway, what about the other leg of your argument, the claim that God would surely ensure a single world religion or set of doctrines? Interestingly, the Christian agrees with you that God will *eventually* secure religious commonality, indeed, *unanimity*, at least where it comes to the most important issues. Where the disagreement lies is in your claim that God would not allow *the degree of religious disagreement we presently witness* prior to the emergence of that future agreement.

And my reply here is that you simply don't know enough about how an omniscient, perfectly good, and maximally wise being would act to justify the claim that this being would be unlikely to actualize a world with the degree of religious disagreement that we presently find.

Justin: Well, I hear you, but let me unpack this premise a bit further.

I want to argue that, if theism is true, we have strong reason to expect believers in God to be in theological agreement (rather than the MTD we observe) at least on the most important issues relating to personal relationship with God. This truth follows by way of unsurpassable divine love and its bias toward meaningful, conscious relationship with her loved ones. Those creatures who currently believe in God have already proven themselves willing and eager for deep divine relationship—it's just that they profoundly disagree with each other on some important issues. God, because she (i) desires her creatures to be in proper relationship with her, (ii) values truth, and

(iii) recognizes that some aspects of theological disagreement can have a negative effect on potential human-divine relationships, can always be expected to prevent widespread disagreement on at least the most important issues.

Randal: Yeah, well I don't see that God would *always* be expected to prevent widespread disagreement. Maybe I can offer an illustration.

Justin: Okay, just make sure this illustration is filled with action, suspense, adventure, and mystery.

Randal: Not a problem. So a few weeks ago I was doing one of those team-building exercises with work colleagues . . .

Justin: You're killing me here, Randal.

Randal: Wait, it gets better! The leader gave us a crisis to overcome and a series of resources to draw upon. Our challenge was to use teamwork to figure out the best way to utilize the resources to meet the crisis. As often happens in exercises like this, we had to weather some disagreement and debate as part of the process. But here's the thing: all that debate served to bring us to the unanimity that emerged only at the end of the exercise. Needless to say, had the leader simply provided us with the full list of proper resources at the beginning, he would have short-circuited the entire team-building process.

On my understanding of God and his action in history, a parallel to this scenario is not only possible, it is highly plausible. In short, we find ourselves with widespread disagreement on particular matters, at least in significant part due to the good of working together in community to try and achieve greater unanimity.

And, in point of fact, that's what you and I are doing right now. The fact that we disagree forces us to reason carefully and listen charitably to each other. And there is value in that journey from disagreement toward agreement. The value isn't limited to the fact that you will eventually admit that I'm right. There is also value in the debate itself.

Justin: I have a bit of a worry here, Randal. So, I want to suggest that this team-builder story you've presented as an analogy is actually a false analogy. There is a hugely relevant difference between the team-building disagreement story and the MTD story playing out around the actual world.

Randal: Did I hear that right? Did you say *false?*

Justin: But it's easily remedied with a modification. This modified version would be one in which you and your colleagues are given a handout stating that there is a crisis of some sort to fix. But in communicating with your colleagues, you find that although they agree that there is, in fact, a crisis of some sort, nevertheless the handouts they've been given assert that the *nature* of the crisis is quite different and requires a very different strategy. Bizarre team-building exercise, I know.

If the leader's purpose in organizing the event really was to encourage teamwork and crisis management, they should be expected to clear up the confusion. Otherwise the event will be nothing more than a perpetual stalemate of disagreement.

Randal: I appreciate your effort but the original analogy works just fine. My point is that a benevolent overseer can have good reasons to allow disagreement on important issues given the intrinsic value in the team-building that comes with communal dialogue and debate.

Moreover, our leader *did* clear up any remaining confusion at the end of the exercise. But when we're talking God's action in history, *we're not yet at the end of the exercise:* we're still in the middle. And I'd say it is presumptuous of you to judge the exercise of theological disagreement in human history as not being worth it when we're very much in the middle and we see things from a terribly limited vantage point. That's like rejecting the value of a day-long team-building exercise after five minutes.

Justin: But Randal, that is fundamentally different. We aren't talking about tying up loose ends of some trivial exercise here. We are talking about fundamental disagreements about the very nature of a much bigger issue about which many people have incompatible beliefs. Moreover, I dare to assume that huge swaths of people didn't die in their ignorance before this team-building exercise was finished and all was revealed.

RELATIONSHIP WITH GOD AND KNOWLEDGE OF GOD

Randal: True, nobody died before the game was over. But Justin, you seem to assume that a meaningful relationship with God is dependent on having the right beliefs about God, from which it follows that all those who have the wrong beliefs about God are thereby precluded from having meaningful relationship with God. I'll grant that if a person holds that assumption, the problem of MTD will seem particularly problematic.

Justin: Okay.

Randal: But here's the thing: no theist is obliged to hold that assumption. On the contrary, it could be that a wide range of people can all be in different degrees of meaningful relationship with God despite having a range of false (and conflicting) beliefs about him.

Justin: Okay, I think I agree, but I'm not entirely sure how this is supposed to be a problem for the argument. Perhaps you could whip up another one of those Rauserian analogies?

Randal: One Rauser analogy coming right up!

So consider the analogy of a child's relationship to her mother. This relationship begins *in utero* when the developing fetus is nurtured by her mother's body and begins to react to the sound of her mother's voice differently from other auditory stimuli. It continues after birth as the baby is breastfed, cradled in her mother's arms, and rocked to sleep. Conscious awareness of her mother is acquired gradually over time, but it emerges out of a prior preconscious relationship, which is itself profound and serves as the basis for that later relationship of awareness.

So one can have knowledge and relationship despite some false beliefs or even with no beliefs.

When one grants this fact, and then adds to it the further possibility that God allows temporary theological disagreement with the intent of achieving a range of substantial goods analogous to the team-building analogy, one finds a substantial rebuttal to your proposed objection.

Justin: Well, hold on, Randal. I'm not entirely sure this rebuttal has the teeth you attribute to it.

I am certainly not disallowing the possibility of nonconscious relationships of the sort that you describe. Of course, God would desire meaningful, *conscious* relationships over other forms of relationship. She would desire this because the previously mentioned rich pool of benefits and values are uniquely available to relationships between two persons (finite and divine) capable of recognizing, appreciating, and interacting with each other. In other words, the goods require a meaningful, conscious relationship.

Secondly, I've not advocated any claim that suggests that, on theism, one must have all and only correct beliefs about God. From the beginning, I've restricted the scope of the relevant disagreements to which this argument refers to theological matters necessary for a conscious and meaningful relationship with God. Therefore, my argument allows for plenty of false beliefs about many other subjects.

Randal: If one need not have correct beliefs about God to be in relationship with God, then many people across the spectrum of theological opinions could be in relationship with God despite their disagreement with each other. And that deals a serious blow to the weight of your objection.

As for my analogy of the fetus/infant in relationship with its mother, it's interesting that you are only willing to grant the mere *possibility* of a relationship here. As a parent who has raised a child, I am confident that the fetus/infant's relationship with her mother is most certainly meaningful—profoundly so. It seems to me that your emphasis on relationship being mediated through correct beliefs suffers from an impoverished vision of relationship.

Justin: Hmm, see I think it's just the opposite. I think it's *you* who are advocating for an impoverished view of relationship.[5]

If a particular relationship is not a conscious two-way street where there is a give and take, a mutual back and forth from the participants, then it's barely worth the label. A fetus without the cognitive hardware for forming the most basic beliefs or making associations is incapable of meaningful relationship.

That said, I do think there is an important distinction to be made here. A parent's *love* for their preconscious fetus may be enormous and meaningful, but the actual *relationship* between the parent and fetus is no more substantive than the "relationship" I have with my favorite pair of shoes.

Randal: I do agree that conscious and cognitive relationships offer the additional value of objectual and propositional knowledge of the one with whom one is in relation. And I believe that those who are in a noncognitive relation with God at present will eventually move into that kind of knowledge just as a noncognitive infant eventually acquires objectual and then propositional knowledge of her mother. However, your claim that the relationship of a mother to her noncognitive or nonverbal infant is no more substantive than your "relationship" with a pair of your shoes is, frankly, bizarre.

Justin: Well, that's just because you haven't walked a mile in my shoes. But more seriously, like my shoes, a preconscious fetus has no awareness of themselves being in a relationship. There is no mutual awareness. There is no substantive interaction.

It's not *just* that conscious relationships offer additional value though. I think that conscious relationships with God specifically make possible a whole swath of additional benefits to finite beings. Benefits include but are not limited to moral strength and valuable experiential knowledge.

Randal: We've been talking about relationships, but what *is* a relationship such that it can be meaningful? A relationship is, minimally, a connection between individuals. There are all sorts of trivial relationships that are not part of our discussion. For example, I have a relationship with every human being on earth in the minimal sense that we all exemplify the same property of being human.

But by focusing on *meaningful* relationships, I take it we mean *existentially* meaningful in that the relationship is somehow formative or constitutive for both persons. And a mother/child relationship surely qualifies here. In a mother/child relationship, each individual shares a profound, existentially definitive connection with the other. This relationship is defined by deep mutual bonding, asymmetric dependence, rich nonverbal communication, and the sharing of complex emotional experiences. It also becomes definitive for the individuals in the relationship. To see that you just need to listen to a mother talk about how she has been changed by motherhood.

Justin: Maybe *that's* where we disagree. Obviously, I do agree with you that a parent and child are capable of a mutual and meaningful relationship when there is mutual awareness (even a nonverbal one), but this capability is not there at *all* stages of fetal development.

Randal: If that were true then a mother's relationship to her anencephalic infant would literally be existentially meaningless. That's outrageous.

But at least you grant that a parent and child *can* have a meaningful nonverbal relationship. That was exactly my point. A fetus/infant is in a meaningful nonverbal or noncognitive relationship with her mother. In the same way, human beings could be in a meaningful nonverbal or noncognitive relationship with God. Indeed, if we understand the God/human relationship to be an analogue for parent/child relationships, then this is to be *expected*. (And in Christian theism it certainly is.) And in that case, (noncognitive) relationship with God may be far more widespread and common than your objection realizes, with its narrow focus on relationship mediated by correct doctrinal propositions.

Justin: Well, I think there is a morally relevant distinction between the relationship that might exist between a parent and their nonverbal toddler and a "relationship" that might exist between a parent and a *preconscious* fetus. I recognize that, while a parent may love their preconscious fetus, the relationship between them and the fetus is not a significant one until that fetus acquires the ability to be aware that it is *actually in a relationship*. Otherwise, as I said, the relationship is of no more value than a relationship with any other object that is not or is not yet a conscious participant.

Randal: To have awareness that one is in a relationship with another requires an awareness of the other, an awareness of oneself, and an awareness of the relatively abstract concept of relationship. If you demand all that, then you will be forced to deny the meaningfulness of relationships with infants, the severely mentally handicapped, and those with advanced dementia and other cognitive deficiencies. (As a dog lover, I also shudder to think what this means for our relationships with Rover, Spot, and Rex.)

Had we more time, I'd love to camp on this debate because I find it fascinating. But I think we need to keep focused on the main issue. An infant lacks propositional knowledge of her mother.

Despite that fact, she can still be in a *profound* relationship with her mother. Don't you agree?

Justin: Well, yes. I think the value of the relationship is sensitive to the cognitive abilities of the persons involved. I think that relationships that are not mutually involved lack substantive value. That may not require propositional knowledge per se, but, in my view, it must involve some form of conscious awareness and appreciation of the other. However, our *love* for these persons or pets need not falter even if the substance of the relationship does.

Let's assume for a moment that the God of Christianity exists. A Muslim may be believing in a God, but their belief is without the proper theological understanding of how to *relate* to God. This limits the potential of relationship simply because of the theological confusion on the ground. Being maximally good, there seems to be no reason why God would not ensure that all capable persons open to a relationship with God would not also be in possession of the essentials for deep, meaningful, and conscious relationship with God. Just as there is no reason for the parent to allow confusion to persist among her children about how best to live, love, or relate to them, the same can be said of a divine parent.

Randal: It seems to me that you're begging the question here by simply assuming that a particular set of propositions about an individual must be believed for one to be in a meaningful relationship with that individual. But the theist need not be bound by that assumption at all. And I've already provided good reasons, sourced in my Christian tradition, why one might question it.

Justin: I've got two things to say here. First, the question in this book is not whether certain historical attachments to theism are in trouble in the face of this argument. The question is what we would expect from basic theism relative to an atheistic hypothesis.

Secondly, the fundamental point here is that a loving God doesn't intentionally keep her loved ones in the dark as to important facts about *how best to have* a conscious and meaningful relationship with them. This will involve the correction of (or a preventing the acquisition of) false beliefs about God among us finite beings, especially as they can foster resentment among tribes with competing theologies.

If we cannot expect at least this of a divine parent, then perhaps the parent in question doesn't deserve the label in the first place.

Randal: Right, let me address those two points then. First, while you're right to note that we are debating a minimal theism, one can defend minimal theism against objections by appealing to particular claims from within a specific theistic tradition. If I can show that theism is consistent with God being in meaningful relationship with folks despite doctrinal disagreement and even in the absence of any propositional knowledge, then that's relevant information to consider in response to the alleged problem of massive theological disagreement.

On the second point, I think you are way too quick to render a judgment. There are all sorts of reasons one might keep a loved one "in the dark." For example, Marcie allows her husband, Joe, to think she's forgotten his birthday precisely because she has an elaborate surprise party planned for later.

Likewise, there are many reasons God may have for allowing current doctrinal disagreements, and I've already outlined some of them. So I just don't see that there is a problem here that need trouble any theist.

Justin: Right, you've previously suggested that one parent might keep their children in the dark as to relationship-relevant facts. This, you've argued, might be a way to address some underlying tensions that already existed between the children.

Randal: Yes, that was one possibility.

COULD GOD GIVE INCOMPATIBLE REVELATIONS?

Justin: Right, so I have a worry here. Allow me to explain what that worry is.

In the various religious traditions in the world, the adherents, or at least the sources from which they draw the content of their beliefs, are said to be divinely inspired. In some sense, they believe that God, through some divine method or other, has *revealed* to them these spiritual truths. That is to say, there is thread attaching their beliefs to their source—God herself. They all believe this to be the case in some fashion.

Am I right to assume you do *not* think that God has given *incompatible revelations* to various people groups?

Randal: No, you would not be right to assume that.

Justin: Ah, well, that's a surprise!

Randal: It shouldn't be.

Justin: Could you go into that a bit more?

Randal: Sure, all one needs to do is keep in mind how any good teacher adjusts their instruction differently for different audiences.

Imagine a science teacher educating a range of students from preschoolers to postgraduate students across a dizzying range of diverse cultures. Do you think that teacher might communicate propositions about nature to a preschooler in one culture that are incompatible with the teaching she provides to a postgraduate student in another culture? Of course, this is *exactly* what you'd expect because every teacher accommodates and contextualizes to their audience.

Likewise, you can expect that God would accommodate and contextualize to various diverse audiences.

Justin: I certainly agree that teachers need to be sensitive to and customize curriculum to the capabilities or culture receiving the information. For example, the teaching metaphors used for a first grade geology class will be very different from those used in classes where students are pursuing a Masters in geology. But I think that is quite different from giving incompatible information. It's not as though the ancients of one religion would be intellectually inferior to the ancients of another (like a child compared to an adult) such that they would require fundamentally different revelations from God.

Randal: Sorry, but I don't think that is correct. Back in first grade, my English teacher taught me "i before e, except after c." Only later did I learn that there's more to that rhyme: "or when sounding like a, as in neighbor or weigh." And any good grammarian knows that even further exceptions apply. These different statements constitute incompatible information. This is one relatively trite example of the movement from technically incorrect accommodation to a more correct understanding, and this kind of movement is common in education. So why couldn't God do something like this in his self-revelation?

Justin: So, Randal, I don't think that any of the ancient cultures who claim to have experienced these revelations were more cognitively advanced than any other. I don't think you do either. Because of that, I don't think that these differences can be explained by way of a comparison between the kinds of oversimplifications we do when teaching children and the more thorough and nuanced teaching we might provide for an adult college student.

Randal: In fact, I think you're wrong here. Different cultures provide access to different concepts and as a result different understandings of God, each with its requisite strengths and weaknesses. So, for example, the Hebrew understanding of God in the Bible is *very* different from the Greek understanding and from that of the contemporary analytic philosopher. Each culture has provided access to a different range of concepts, and in each case God has accommodated to that culture as any good teacher would.

Justin: I understand that the world as we know it has varied understandings of God. The question I'm after is why these concepts were allowed to persist in the first place rather than being corrected.

In any case, you can probably tell that my point in bringing this up is that, in the story of the parents allowing disagreement to persist in hopes to address underlying tensions, the disagreement had to come from somewhere. If the story is to be relevant to the argument at hand, the conflicting information had to come from the parents themselves. In other words, there is misinformation being given in order to address an underlying tension. There seems to be something less than morally perfect about that kind of problem-solving strategy. I think the same problem applies to any God who tells various ancient cultures conflicting information (lying) and allows the disagreement to persist for some end.

Randal: Accommodating instruction to an audience is not "lying." The English teacher who instructs her grade one students "i before e, except after c" as if this were an exceptionless norm does not thereby "lie" to them.

Justin: Perhaps not. That said, revealing to one ancient tribe that Jesus died and rose on the third day while revealing to another that Jesus was but a mere prophet *would* be lying. It seems remarkably improbable that an omnipotent being wouldn't be able to find a better way to address whatever underlying issue needs addressing without lying to and confusing his children for thousands of years.

Randal: I think the issues with pedagogy and truthful witness are far more complicated than you're recognizing. Anyway, I don't believe God revealed to anybody that Jesus is a mere prophet, so people who come to believe that are mistaken. The bottom line here is that God acts as a master teacher who reveals aspects of himself and his will in different ways and to different degrees in accord with the myriad of distinct cultural contexts, individual capacities, and particular needs of the target audience.

Justin: We're talking about an omnipotent and morally perfect God here. It seems to me that, if God could accomplish this task *without* thousands of years of deception and confusion, she would.

Randal: Once again, it isn't deception. To show that it is, you'd need to have independent knowledge that God was intending to deceive rather than contextualize information to a particular audience.

Perhaps it is time to underscore the point that one can be in a propositional relationship with another individual despite believing some incorrect propositions about that individual. For example, a husband and wife may have a profound relationship despite the fact that the husband is a government spy rather than the carpet salesman that his wife had been led to believe. One might believe the husband had morally sufficient reasons (e.g., national security, the safety of his spouse) to allow his wife to hold those false beliefs. That does not change the fact that their relationship is real and important.

Justin: Right, but notice that nothing about that scenario you've presented keeps substantive relationship out of the reach of the wife and husband. Theists all over have very different and incompatible views about the nature of God, how *best* to relate with God, how *best* to please God, and how *best* to live. The wife and husband don't have *those* kinds of problems.

Now, if the actual world is in fact a theistic world, most theists are just dead wrong about many of these questions simply because, statistically, they have subscribed to the wrong theology—a false theology that God, if she exists, has allowed to persist among her children for thousands of years. A loving parent would want all their children to know the basic facts about how *best* to enter relationship with their parent at all moments in which the child is capable of such relationship.

Theologically, I should think you'd agree with me here. It's widely held that God, if she exists, would never force a relationship on any resistant person. This is because the most meaningful relationships (like those we'd expect to exist between God and a willing finite creature) are entered into *freely* by willing and aware participants.

Randal: I agree that God wouldn't force a relationship. But I find it interesting that you understand the most meaningful relationships to be those that maximize personal autonomy. It seems to me that the mother/child bond I've described is among the most profound and meaningful of relationships. And yet, it is a relationship into which one of the parties always enters without any free assent. (No child chooses to be conceived and born.) But it is no less existentially meaningful for that fact.

Justin: Like I said, I think the most meaningful relationships are those in which both persons are aware of the other and capable of interacting intentionally with each other. I also think that, all else being equal, relationships entered into freely by both parties are better than those that exist by default.

I'm beginning to see that our respective intuitions about what a morally perfect God would or would not do with respect to theological disagreement are in radical opposition. I hope that I've at least shown that arguments of this sort, which appeal to facts-on-the-ground about theistic belief, can be serious arguments.

DOCTRINE AND SALVATION

Randal: At the very least, I think you've done that. You *have* shown that these arguments are serious. Though I've done my best to *limit* your success in that regard! But there is no doubt that this is a family of arguments that presents a very serious prima facie objection to theistic belief.

That said, before we move on perhaps I can say a brief word about the first of your final two concerns, namely the fact that many people, perhaps *billions*, have died with a lack of theological understanding. While I'm inclined to agree with you, I believe that from a Christian perspective there's even *more* confusion than one might initially think. But I also suspect that may not be quite as bad as it looks.

Justin: Interesting. Go on.

Randal: Consider the case of Thomas Aquinas. Widely considered the greatest of medieval theologians and author of such monumental academic treatises as *Summa Theologiae* and *Summa Contra Gentiles*, one would think that if anyone knew God, it'd be Thomas. However, while attending Mass on December 6, 1273, Thomas underwent some sort of mystical experience, after which he resolved never to write another word of theology. As he explained to his assistant, Brother Reginald, "I can't go on. . . . Everything seems as so much straw in comparison with what I have seen and what has been revealed to me."[6]

The lesson here is not that theological theories are worthless, but rather that they utterly pale in comparison with the reality they purport to describe. To consider an analogy from natural science, imagine a crude model of the solar system comprised of various foam balls hung on wires in a grade-school classroom. A child might think they understand the solar system well because they understand that model. And the model *does* have value, as it offers a map, however crude and limited, of our cosmic backyard. But imagine now that the same child boards a spaceship with Neil deGrasse Tyson and takes a tour of the solar system. After she gets back to the classroom, she'll never look at that model the same way again! Useful though it may be, when compared with the solar system it is "so much straw."

Justin: In all honesty, Randal, there are *much* easier ways of revealing to me that my amazing second-grade science project won me a spaceship tour of the solar system with Neil deGrasse Tyson. I mean, really, that was needlessly elaborate.

Randal: What can I say? I do love spinning a good tale!

Here's the thing: on that December day in 1273, Thomas may have come to terms with the gap between his models and God. But along the way, he also *experienced* God in a new way that transcended his inadequate straw models.

I suspect that much of the massive theological disagreement that exists across various conceptions of God is borne by the inadequacy of our models. But, like Thomas, the path is open to every person to *experience* God in a way that transcends their theology. The massive theological disagreement that drives your argument is not the final word.

Justin: Well, that's an interesting story. I just worry that it doesn't interact much with the main thrust of my argument. We've gone back and forth discussing how likely or unlikely the massive range of theological disagreement among those who self-identify as theists is on our competing hypotheses of theism and atheism. I still think that it's just obvious that the fact of massive theological disagreement provides significant support to the hypothesis that there is no loving God to keep her children from widespread confusion of the sort relevant to deep, meaningful two-way relationships.

But, of course, that's where we have our own little theological disagreement.

Randal: Hah, yes, on that we agree.

Chapter 4

GOD AND MORAL OBLIGATION

Randal: You know, I've got a feeling we could keep hashing out the issue of theological disagreement all day.

Justin: Hmm, I think you're probably right about that.

Randal: So is it alright with you if we shift gears? I've got one or two arguments for God up my proverbial sleeve, and I'd like to hear what you think.

Justin: Sure thing. Let's see what you got.

SETTING UP THE MORAL QUESTIONS

Randal: Great! Remember I promised to talk about arguments that would distinguish God from your maximally evil being. It's time to make good on that promise.

Justin: Good. Let's hear it.

Randal: So what I'm thinking about right now is how best to explain an aspect of morality.

Justin: There are plenty of aspects to morality. What specifically are you after?

Randal: Ahh, a very practical question! So, as you know, morality is concerned both with moral value and moral obligation. Moral value deals with questions of good and evil, while moral obligation deals with questions of right and wrong, ought and ought not.

Justin: A hugely important distinction!

Randal: Indeed it is.

Any comprehensive account of moral value should seek to explain the origin of good and evil: why does our universe include these moral properties? And any account of moral obligation should seek to explain the origin and nature of right and wrong. That is,

99

why is one act morally right and another act morally wrong? In other words, why is it that I *ought* to do x but I *ought not* do y?

Justin: I think this is right in so far as we assume moral statements are cognitive. Assuming moral statements to be cognitive means we assume that moral statements express propositions that can be objectively true or false about the world. Some persons deny this, and they are called noncognitivists.

Randal: Good point. Indeed, this would be a good time to say something about *moral semantics.* Semantics is concerned with meaning. And thus, moral semantics is concerned with what it *means* to make moral utterances like "Rape is wrong" or "Compassion is good." The noncognitivist will deny that these seemingly meaningful expressions succeed in conveying a proposition that is true or false. For example, in ethical emotivism all moral statements are interpreted as emotional expressions like "Boo! Rape!" and "Yah! Compassion!"

But I'm guessing you're not a noncognitivist, right?

Justin: That's correct. I think moral judgments like this convey something more than mere boos, hisses, or cheers. That said, plenty of atheists are noncognitivists and their arguments are interesting and worth considering.

Randal: Agreed. Or should I say, I can *cheer* that! So let's turn back to moral values and obligations. Consider the two statements "Murder is wrong" (a statement of moral value) and "You ought not murder" (a statement of moral obligation). What is the truthmaker of these statements? That is, what is it that makes it *true* that murder is wrong and that you ought not murder?

Justin: Correct me if I'm wrong here, but are those statements not true in virtue of their definitions? In other words, is it not the very meaning of the word "murder" that makes it wrong and its wrongness that requires that we should not murder? That's at least how it seems to me.

Randal: Excellent point, Justin! You're right that the word "murder" just means *unjustified killing.* Consider the statement "All bachelors are unmarried." Since "bachelor" just *means* "an unmarried male of marrying age," it follows trivially that all bachelors are unmarried. And, likewise, since murder just is "unjustified killing," it follows trivially that all murder is wrong.

Justin: Okay, great. That point aside, it was clear that we're after something more substantive with your question. It had something to do with trying to understand what distinguishes right from wrong and the obligations that follow from those distinctions.

Randal: Right. What I want to do is get past the semantic convention to arrive at the moral values and moral obligations behind our condemnation of murderous acts. Perhaps the best way to do this is to give a concrete description of a particular action.

So, consider this: on the battlefield in WW2, a Nazi surrenders to an English soldier, Private Killum. While Killum has the capacity to take the Nazi as a prisoner, he instead decides to torture, kill, and mutilate the Nazi. We judge Killum's actions to be immoral. But why? What is it that makes them immoral? What is the nature of the values and obligations that he has flouted in torturing, killing, and mutilating the hapless Nazi POW?

You and I both need to provide an account of the moral evil of Private Killum's actions and the violation of moral obligation that he commits when performing them. And my claim is going to be that theism offers distinct advantages over atheism in explaining both moral value and moral obligation.

But I take it you disagree. So can you explain how *you* understand the nature of moral value and moral obligation?

Justin: That certainly helps. To be clear, both theists and atheists have endorsed a variety of positions on these metaethical and applied ethics questions and so I do want to be clear that the position I'll be forwarding here is but *one of many* possible options for the atheist. It just so happens that the view to which I subscribe is available to both theists and atheists alike.

Now, according to desirism, a view that I find plausible,[1] in order to make progress in answering this question, we need first to ask a different question. Would a person with good desires do that which was attributed to Private Killum? If a person with good desires would *not* do the act that Private Killum has done in that situation, then that act is *morally impermissible.*

Randal: Okay, but let's be sure to keep in mind that we need to explain *two* things: moral value and moral obligation. By torturing, killing, and mutilating the Nazi, Private Killum commits acts of moral *dis-*

value. In other words, those actions are *evil*. Moreover, Killum has a moral obligation not to perform those evil actions. Thus, when he engages in evil, he performs actions that violate his moral obligations not to perform evil.

INTRODUCING ETHICS AND DESIRE

Justin: Ah yes, I've left out the *value* aspect of your question. As an aside, not all theories make that value/obligation distinction. For me though, I'll need to unpack some foundational aspects first. I hold that value terms like *good* or *bad* describe relationships. Specifically, they describe relationships between desires and states of affairs. So I want to say that values are actually relational properties. Notice that relational properties (like distance to or from) are things that we can be right or wrong about. They aren't mere matters of opinion.

Randal: I think I follow you. But can you unpack it a bit more?

Justin: Sure. Maybe an illustration will help. Tom has an aversion to (a desire to avoid) pain. Tom lives his life like most of us trying to avoid unnecessary pain. One day, Tom accidentally stubs his toe, causing him a few moments of extreme pain. At that moment, Tom's aversion to pain is being thwarted by the state of affairs of his toe slamming into a step causing him pain. Another way to say this is that the relationship between his desire not to feel pain and the state of affairs that is his feeling pain are in direct conflict. This is *bad*. While it is Tom's subjective state of mind feeling the pain, the relationship between his feeling pain and his desire to not be feeling pain is directly and objectively in conflict. Given that Tom has a desire to avoid pain, he has a strong reason to walk more cautiously, so he *should* walk more cautiously.

Randal: Okay, I get the reasoning thus far, but I'm not sure this is going to get you where you want to go.

Justin: That's certainly understandable, as I've only really addressed value generically. You've expressed interest in my views on specifically *moral* value. I hold that *moral* value is a subcategory of value, just like orchids are a subcategory of flowering plants. Recall that this view holds that values describe the relationship between desires and states of affairs. Well, for moral values, we are focusing on relationships between desires and *specific kinds* of states of affairs—mainly states of the brain. Other desires! So, moral value is concerned with relationships between desires.

Now, not all desires are created equal. Some desires are "good" desires in that they are desires that people generally have many strong reasons to promote in their world. Other desires are "bad" desires in that they are desires that people generally have many strong reasons to discourage in their world.

Remember when I said earlier that if a person with good desires would *not* do the act that Private Killum has done in that situation then that act is *morally impermissible*?

Randal: I do indeed remember that.

Justin: This is what I was getting at. We should be assessing the desire(s) at the root of Private Killum's act. Was it a good desire? Would a person with good desires—those desires that people generally have reason to promote—do what Private Killum has done?

If not, he has done an impermissible act.

DEBATING DESIRISM

Randal: Good, thanks for the quick overview of your understanding of moral value. Let's hash this out for a bit before we turn to discussing moral obligation.

If I understand your view correctly, moral value exists when actions are undertaken based on particular kinds of reason.

Justin: The view I'm defending here says that value simply exists as a relationship between values and states of affairs. These exist independently of whether any action is ever actually motivated by them. Obviously, in the actual world, desires motivate people to act all the time.

Randal: Yes, well I have a couple of responses to this. First, we can often act in a way that is *pretheoretical* such that it does not involve any reasoning from premise to conclusion. It would seem that, on your view, these kinds of actions are not ripe for moral appraisal because they are not undertaken with explicit ends in mind. Is this correct?

Justin: It's certainly true that many of our actions are done without explicit appeal to reasoning or desires. But I think it's important to realize that, just because an action is done without careful consideration, it does not mean that it was not motivated by some combination of desires and beliefs. All intentional actions require at least one belief and one desire. So long as a desire is involved in the act in question, it's fair game for moral evaluation.

Randal: So would you say that the reasoning that makes an action ripe for moral appraisal need not be explicit? It can also be tacit or implicit?

Justin: What I mean to say is that, in so far as the action in question is intentional (motivated by a desire), it is appropriate to evaluate morally. Think of it this way: we don't live in a vacuum. We also don't often have access to what desires people have—at least not until their actions reveal them. Obviously, we hope that those around us have those kinds of desires that people generally have many and strong reasons to promote. But why is this? It's because that person's intentional actions will, by definition, be motivated by the desires they have. Whether the desires were being consciously considered or bubbling in the background at the time of the act in question doesn't matter much.

Randal: Okay, thanks for filling out the picture a bit more. To come to my second point, I want to take a closer look at Private Killum. You see, he could have many reasons for torturing, killing, and mutilating the Nazi. And those were in keeping with his desires. Could those actions possibly be morally right on your view? Could they be among the "many and strong reasons" you refer to that can inform morality? And if not, why not?

Justin: I'm not sure I'm completely clear on what your question is. Could you give an example of what you mean here?

Randal: Sure. Private Killum kills the Nazi because that is more likely to ensure his own survival, and he not surprisingly values his own life over that of the anonymous Nazi. As for the torturing and mutilating, those seemingly cruel actions are borne of Killum's desire to objectify and depersonalize his victim, with the intent that this will minimize the adverse psychological consequences he will later experience for having performed the killing. Those are reasons informed by Killum's desire for his own safety and personal happiness. Are they sufficient to make his actions moral?

In other words, what are the criteria by which you distinguish morally right desires and reasons from morally evil ones?

Justin: Oh, okay. I think I see what you're after now. So, what we need to do is ask if the desire to torture/kill/dehumanize/etc. others is a desire that we generally have many strong reasons to promote in our world. It seems to me that dehumanizing others, especially for justifying some future killing, is not the kind of desire that we generally have reasons to promote. Hopefully that helps!

Randal: Alas, I'm not sure it does. After all, you might generally have reasons not to promote a desire for something, and yet find yourself in a specific situation where it *is* advisable to promote it. For example, generally I don't have reasons to push a granny from behind, but if that is the only way to save her from getting run over by a bus then I'll do it.

Justin: Ah, so here you've identified a situation in which two *good* desires seemingly conflict. On the one hand, we all (granny included) generally have many strong reasons to promote an aversion to (a desire to avoid) infringing on other people's bodily autonomy. On the other hand, we *all* (granny included) generally have many strong reasons to promote an aversion to letting others needlessly die.

What's important to notice here is that, just because both desires are *good*, it does not follow that they are *equally* good. Some *good* desires really are such that we generally have more and stronger reasons to promote one over the other. In the example of these two competing desires, we generally have more and stronger reasons to promote an aversion to letting people needlessly die than we have reasons to promote an aversion to infringing on another's bodily autonomy. After all, without our lives, bodily autonomy wouldn't matter.

Randal: I'm not so sure about your analysis. I don't think I would know in advance whether Granny would value her life more than her autonomy. Indeed, she might be *angry* at me for saving her life, despite my best intentions. Maybe she just wanted to end it all.

Justin: That is certainly possible, but notice I've never said that we should know every detail of our specific circumstances before acting. That would be an impossible standard for any moral theory to impose upon moral agents. All I've said is that people *generally* have many strong reasons for action for promoting an aversion to needless death *more so* than an aversion to invasions of bodily autonomy. This is true even if there may be exceptions.

UNQUALIFIED MORAL JUDGMENTS

Randal: I still disagree. In the crisis moment, I may have *no idea* about the range of reasons for a particular action, but I still know that I need to act.

Regardless, let's leave those details aside and get back to Private Killum. You see, I don't think that his decision to torture, kill, and mutilate the Nazi POW could *ever* be morally justified. Those actions are not like pushing a granny from behind to save her life. Torture and mutilation are intrinsically dehumanizing actions. Those actions are *always wrong*. They're *evil*.

Do you agree? And if you do, how do you justify an *unqualified* condemnation of Private Killum's actions based on your moral framework?

Justin: While I'm not wedded to the need for an unqualified condemnation, I see no reason why this view is incapable of joining you in an unqualified condemnation of Private Killum's actions. Recall that the view states that if a good person (a person with all good desires) would never intentionally do the act in question, then the act in question is morally impermissible and inexcusable. I think it is quite clear that no good person would do the acts you've claimed for the fictional private.

Randal: In my view it certainly is clear that it is always wrong to torture, kill, and mutilate the POW. For all the difficult cases one encounters in the moral life, there are nonetheless many other cases in which an ethical judgment is clear and unqualified, and to my mind this is one of them.

Justin: I think we're largely in agreement here.

Randal: I don't know about that. In the ethic you've presented, ethical judgment consists of weighing the distribution of reasons for and against a desire to perform an action and that is far more nebulous than an intuitive grasp of intrinsic evils.

Justin: I don't see how this is any less nebulous than discussing God. It seems to me that, while we might not be able to be as exacting with our conceptual and empirical considerations as to what effect any particular desire tends to have on others, that shouldn't be seen as a fatal flaw. For it seems quite obvious to me that the desire to rape, for example, is a desire that, when introduced into a community, will tend to thwart desires, while a desire for charity will tend to fulfill them.

Randal: Actions like rape thwart some desires, but they also satisfy other desires. That's why people rape, because they have particular desires (e.g., domination, violence, sexual gratification, etc.). What you need is an *immediate* judgment that can condemn particular desires unequivocally, one that can thereby justify the immediate way that properly functioning and moral people condemn such clear and egregious moral violations as the act of rape.

So let me lay my cards on the table: can you state with conviction and immediacy that Private Killum's torture, killing, and mutilation of the POW was unequivocally wrong, that such behavior is *always* wrong? If so, how do you *justify* that judgment? If not, then when is the torture, killing, and mutilation of POWs morally good?

Justin: Yes (with conviction and immediacy), Killum's torture, killing, and mutilation of the POW was morally wrong.

Now, when I say that Killum's behavior was morally wrong, I mean to draw attention to the fact that Killum did those things *because* some of his desires were the exact kinds of desires we generally have many strong reasons to condemn and weaken in ourselves and in others. They tend to *thwart* other desires. They are *bad* desires.

A person with *good* desires simply would not intentionally treat the POW in that way. On this view then, Killum's actions are clearly morally impermissible.

MORAL PERCEPTION

Randal: Okay, thanks for that. I'm glad you agree that Killum's actions are unequivocally wrong. However, I still find your explanation for *why* they are wrong and what it *means* for them to be wrong to be nebulous and thus deeply unsatisfactory.

You condemn Killum's actions because they are at odds with the kinds of desires we have many strong reasons to promote. But a person can have many strong reasons to promote desires that are nonetheless *evil.* It's a truism that *every* desire has the potential to thwart other desires. An account of morality must explain why some desires are good and thus rightly acted upon, while others are evil, and thus rightly thwarted.

You see, my take is very different. While I acknowledge cases of moral deliberation, where we must reason to the right course of action, I also believe that we can simply perceive that some particular kinds of actions are good and others are evil. And Killum's actions (torture, murder, and mutilation) are evil.

Now let me address the epistemological elephant in my ethical room: how can I claim to know these kinds of moral facts in this immediate and unequivocal way? Simple: because I believe human beings have a faculty of moral perception that allows them to perceive moral facts as surely as sense perception allows us to perceive sense perceptible facts.

Justin: Hmm, interesting. What part or parts of the human brain house this moral-grasping faculty?

Randal: I don't know. But, then, keep in mind that I also don't know which parts of the human brain "house" the faculty of rational intuition or memory or sense perception. Our knowledge of the brain, the most complex structure in the known universe, is very limited and very much in flux. Fortunately, a person doesn't need to know *how* rational intuition or memory or sense perception or moral perception functions to know *that* each of these faculties provides knowledge.

Justin: Good point.

Randal: How about I give you a real world example of this immediate moral perception at work?

Justin: That might help.

Randal: Sure thing. When the great Russian novelist Leo Tolstoy visited Paris, he witnessed a public execution by beheading. He later wrote the following reflection on his experience:

When I saw the head divided from the body and heard the sound with which it fell separately into the box, I understood, not with my reason, but with my whole being, that no theory of the wisdom of all established things, nor of progress, could justify such an act; and that if all the men in the world from the day of creation, by whatever theory, had found this thing necessary, it was not so; it was a bad thing, and that therefore I must judge of what was right and necessary, not by what men said and did, not by progress, but what I felt to be true in my heart.[2]

Of course, people can disagree with Tolstoy about the wrongness of public executions. So my claim is not that moral perception is infallible. (Nor is that surprising, since *none* of our cognitive faculties are infallible.)

Rather, my main point in this example is to bring out the immediacy and bracing moral conviction with which people form basic moral assessments. Just as a person can immediately intuit rationally that $2 + 2 = 4$ through their rational faculties, and just as they can immediately sense-perceive that the sun is shining by seeing the sun shining, so they can immediately perceive that a particular action is good or evil, right or wrong, through their moral perception of the action (either by witnessing it or contemplating it). This knowledge isn't produced by weighing various desires in a deliberative fashion. Rather, as with Tolstoy's judgment, these kinds of moral convictions are *immediate* and acquired *prior to deliberation*.

THE PROBLEM OF CHANGING MORAL PERCEPTION

Justin: Hmm, well I certainly wouldn't want to undermine a kind of immediate intuition as a way of knowing *some* things. Such a view would be untenable. On the view you've forwarded though, how would one go about explaining massive shifts over time in moral sentiment? The dramatic shift in attitudes about homosexuality comes to mind.

Randal: Go on.

Justin: With few exceptions, homosexuality was *perceived* as *obviously* morally wrong in an *immediate* way for many of the earth's population. Its wrongness was as obvious to them as the wrongness of beheading was for Tolstoy. Setting aside the question of whether each individual would be rational in trusting their perception, a different but related question naturally pops up. How are we to explain shifts like this on a view like yours?

Randal: Good question, Justin. Attitudes over time *have* changed on countless issues. Homosexuality is one issue. One could add many other topics as well, like slavery, cannibalism, polygamy, women's rights, and capital punishment—as in Tolstoy's horror at a public beheading.

Indeed, the topic of capital punishment brings me to what is literally one particularly painful example: *torture*. When I was a kid thirty years ago, I visited Madame Tussauds Wax Museum in London. For a thirteen year old kid like me, the most memorable exhibit was the Chamber of Horrors. Seeing devices like the horrifying pear of anguish and breaking wheel fascinated and repulsed me. Those wax recreations haunted my imagination for years to come: I couldn't imagine how human beings could inflict such horrors on one another. Today, people widely agree that it is morally wrong to torture people in the manner of these cruel devices. But here's the obvious question: if we have an ability to perceive moral facts with immediacy as I've claimed, then how could some folks get things so wrong?

To start with, let me say that my disagreement with the medievals on this issue doesn't shake *my* conviction that torture is wrong. On this score, I'm with Tolstoy: By whatever theory others have found the pear of anguish to be morally justified, I insist that it was not so; it was a bad thing, and therefore, like Tolstoy, I too must judge of what is right and necessary, not by what men said or did, not by progress, but by what *I* feel to be true in my heart. In other words, I believe that those medievals who tortured people were *wrong* and that what they did was *evil*. And I am responsible to my conscience.

Justin: Okay, I can understand that. However, I think I am more interested in how these facts are explained on your view. Presumably, you want to say both that we've been given a faculty of moral perception and that this faculty is generally reliable.

For example, our perception of temperature may fail under certain circumstances, but we have good reasons to think it generally reliable. It's not as though the temperature perceptions of people living hundreds of years ago had them believing that fire was actually cold and ice hot! Shouldn't we think that *moral* perception, if it operates similarly in all persons, would not differ so dramatically from culture to culture and from ancient to present times?

Randal: Hah! I like that illustration.

For starters, as I said, while moral perception may be immediate, it isn't *infallible*. Sometimes intuitions can be mistaken. For example, our moral perception can malfunction based on cultural conditioning or the distorting influence of personal prejudice. The sober lesson here is that moral perception can *misfire*, so to speak.

Second, even when moral perception is working fine, we might *deny the moral knowledge we have*. For example, when Hutus hunted down and butchered their Tutsi neighbors during the Rwandan genocide, I think at some level they *knew* what they were doing was wrong and evil. But they were *rationalizing* their behavior by dehumanizing their Tutsi neighbors and calling them *cockroaches*. Countless genocides have been carried out on these terms, with the genocidaires suppressing their own knowledge of the evil of their actions.

So I am okay with saying that moral perception is fallible and that we can choose to disregard the deliverances of our moral perception. Neither of these facts undermines my general conviction that moral perception can provide knowledge. Nor do they undermine my conviction that torture is *wrong* based simply on moral reflection on the act of torture.

Justin: We agree that, if there is a faculty that works in this way, it would be fallible, just as we agree that other faculties, like vision or temperature perception, are fallible. But to bring back my other point, other faculties don't seem to differ in their outputs nearly as dramatically over time or across cultural borders as our moral values do. People in the first century didn't mistake an elephant for a tree more often than do modern persons.

Randal: You got me there! I never heard of anybody mistaking a pachyderm for a ponderosa pine.

Justin: Given this difference, would you say we should be less confident in our ability to perceive moral truths than we are in our ability to perceive the world around us visually?

Randal: No, I don't agree. Tell me, Justin, are you *more* persuaded that the sky is blue than that it is wrong to torture infants and rape women for fun?

Justin: Good point. At least *some* moral truths are as obvious as the sky is blue. But, then again, those moral truths are as obvious to me as the fact that human slavery is wrong, and yet your view of moral perception doesn't seem very well equipped to explain the gradual correction here.

THE FACULTY OF MORAL PERCEPTION AND DESIRES

Randal: On the contrary, my view of moral perception fully allows for a diversity of opinion to emerge, for the reasons I've already noted. At the same time, we have a situation where we seem to perceive particular moral facts with the same unavoidable immediacy that we perceive rational axioms or sense perceptual facts. I can just *see* that $2 + 2 = 4$ and that the sky is blue, and I can just *see* that particular actions are morally good and praiseworthy and others are morally evil and condemnable.

This amazing faculty of moral perception is no surprise to me. After all, I believe God is morally perfect and wants his creatures to gain moral knowledge about the world and to act on it accordingly. So I would expect human beings to be furnished with a cognitive faculty to provide moral knowledge.

But where does this faculty of moral perception come from, in your view? It seems to be a fundamentally mysterious ability on atheism, no?

Justin: In my view, what we're perceiving isn't some kind of intrinsic essence of goodness or badness in certain behaviors. Rather, we're perceiving the motivations behind those actions as being desires that are clearly the kinds of desires that tend to thwart other desires.

Randal: As I already observed, every desire thwarts some other desires, so that is not a helpful criterion for identifying moral properties.

What makes an action moral or immoral is not whether the action thwarts desires but rather whether it is good or evil. These are primal concepts. They are part of the furniture of the universe, so to speak. Good and evil are as surely a part of the world as the shape and texture of material objects. Just as our sense perception can perceive the shape and texture of material objects, so our moral perception perceives the good and evil of particular actions.

If I walk into an alley and see a woman being raped, I don't know what the rapist's desires are. He could have many different desires that lead him to rape. (And as I pointed out, the same is true of Private Killum's murderous actions.) But I don't need to have access to the rapist's mental states to know that he is engaged in an action that is morally evil. So, unlike you, I *do* believe that actions like rape are intrinsically evil.

Justin: It's of course true that *every* desire potentially thwarts *some* other desire. But that is no objection to a view that states that desires are to be evaluated as to the *tendency* with which they relate to other desires. We can still say the desire to rape is a bad desire—a desire that a good person would not have—because it tends to thwart other desires.

Alonzo Fyfe, the primary defender of this view, writes,

> We can see the problem with the desire to rape by imagining that we have control over a knob that will generally increase or decrease the intensity and spread of a desire to rape throughout a community. To the degree that we increase this desire to rape, to that degree we increase the desires that will be thwarted. Either the desires of the rapist will have to be thwarted, or the desires of the victims will have to be thwarted. The more and stronger the desire to rape, the more and stronger the desires that will be thwarted.[3]

Randal: Okay, and . . . ?

Justin: Well, let's apply Fyfe's knob-themed thought experiment to the desire for charity. What if we were to turn up a fictional knob associated with the desire to do charity such that it increases the intensity and spread of a desire to do charity throughout a community? My point is that not all desires are created equal.

Randal: But once again I come to the point that the thwarting of desires is, in itself, neither here nor there. Everything depends on the *moral status* of the desires being thwarted. Let's say you become convinced that it is wrong to eat sentient animals. By becoming an active defender of vegetarianism, you turn the dial way up so that it will thwart all sorts of desires people have for hamburgers and pepperoni pizza and chicken wings. But, if it is morally wrong to kill and eat other sentient creatures simply because we enjoy the taste, then this moral fact trumps and thwarts an entire buffet of culinary desires.

Justin: If you turn up the dial associated with the desire for a vegetarian diet though, you are simultaneously eliminating or lessening the desire for diets that include meat. Notice that the desire for a vegetarian diet isn't a desire that tends to thwart other desires. It makes more sense then, to turn up *that* dial than to turn up the dial that will tend to thwart other desires.

Randal: I beg to differ. One can desire a vegetarian diet for moral reasons while desiring meat for taste.

Justin: Well, okay, but I hope you see my point. Anyway, it's clear that we conceive of morality in entirely different ways, but it's not at all clear that theism somehow constitutes a superior view in regard to the specific question of how we come to *know* moral facts. On your view, moral facts are basic and are perceived directly. On my view, moral facts are just facts about desires and their relationships to each other.

Randal: That's not quite my view. I certainly do believe that we *all* directly perceive basic moral facts, but that doesn't mean that *all* the moral facts we perceive are basic. Some are the result of careful deliberation. And that's part of the reason that we need ethical theories: they help us organize and justify our respective moral deliberations.

Nonetheless, a significant amount of our moral knowledge is indeed basic and thus immediate. If a properly functioning person sees a rape in progress, they don't need to reason to the conclusion that the act is wrong by undertaking a calculation based on the projected thwarting of various desires. They know absolutely and unequivocally that it is *wrong*. We can leave the moral philosophers to develop theories of the nature of morality. But the starting point of moral knowledge itself is *immediate* and *pretheoretical.* That's the nature of our moral condemnation of Private Killum's torture, murder, and mutilation of his hapless POW as well. And I don't see that your desirist theory can explain this type of knowledge.

Justin: I've claimed the initial evaluation of desires is deliberative, but that is a separate issue from the fact that, once a person is driven by good desires, deliberation won't be necessary for acts. They will do the right thing naturally. That kind of automatic goodness of action is what we want from those around us.

Randal: I can see we're not going to agree here. Before we move on to a completely new topic, I'd like to say something about another aspect of morality that I believe favors theism. Are you okay with that?

Justin: But yes, we're unlikely to resolve this difference in our views here. What other aspect of morality were you interested in discussing?

MORAL OBLIGATION AND MORAL CALLING

Randal: I want to come back to moral obligation—the sense that we are obliged to do particular actions and obliged to refrain from doing other actions.

To give a sense of what I'm thinking, perhaps I can begin with the case of John Rabe, a German businessman working in Nanjing, China, in 1937. By September, it was becoming clear that the advancing Japanese army was about to take over the city. Given the notorious reputation of the Japanese for brutality, the obvious course of action beckoned: flee the war-torn country by retreating to the safety of the West. But against every impulse of his nature, Rabe resolved to stay. In his journal, as presented in the 2007 documentary *Nanking*, he offered the following reason why:

> Under such circumstances can I, may I, cut and run? I don't think so. Anyone who has ever sat in the dugout and held a trembling Chinese child in each hand through the long hours of an air raid can understand what I feel. The rich are fleeing, the poor remain behind. They don't know where to go. They don't have the means to flee. Aren't they in danger of being

slaughtered in great numbers? Shouldn't one make an attempt to help them? There's a question of morality here. And so far, I haven't been able to sidestep it.[4]

Rabe is right: there *is* a question of morality here. More specifically, there is a question of moral *obligation* and, perhaps even more provocatively, of *moral calling*. It's the experience of recognizing in particular moments a deep moral claim upon our lives, an obligation and perhaps a specific calling to act in a particular way, even when doing so frustrates our personal interest and desires.

Justin: Interesting. I don't experience moral obligation as some kind of *external* calling. I experience it as a collection of particular kinds of reasons I have for acting. Obviously, I have reasons for doing all sorts of things—jogging, going to sleep, or engaging in conversation. The question is, what is the difference between generic reasons and *moral* reasons. In my view, the difference is that generic reasons are not the kinds of reasons that people generally have strong reasons to promote or condemn in any significant way. Moral reasons, on the other hand, are.

Randal: It seems like you view moral obligation as nothing more than the end result of a moral calculation weighing reasons for and against a particular action. But that's not the way it is.

Justin: Well, I do have to disagree with your loaded wording here. The view I'm endorsing here is that an obligatory act is the act that a person with all good desires *would* do under those particular circumstances. And there need not always be a careful mathematical calculation involved—after all, a person with good desires (and the right balance of them) will just naturally attempt the obligatory act because it is what they *want* to do.

Randal: Your explanation misses the core issue: while an obligatory act is one a person with good desires would do, they'd do the act *because it is obligatory*. And it is this moral obligation that you need to explain.

Justin: I must admit that I can make no sense of this. Presumably when you say a particular act is *obligatory*, you mean that there exists a moral sort of possibly indefeasible reasons to do that act, regardless of whether these reasons are consciously being entertained or sit in the background as one's moral character. When somebody acts on those kinds of reasons, they are doing acts that are morally obligatory. Maybe you conceive of moral obligation as some sort of magical force out there, but I just see no reason to grant your profound certitude on this matter any weight at all.

Now, if you think moral obligations are acts done divorced from reasons for action, or if you think that there exist reasons for action that do *not* boil down to desires, I'm all ears.

Randal: I said nothing about indefeasibility or "profound certitude," still less a "magical force." But moral obligation is indeed a feature of the moral life. If the mundane facts of reasoning are black, white, and gray, the call to moral action is bracing technicolor. In these particular moments, we experience a grip on our lives that can obliterate our moral calculus. For example, without a second thought, we dive into the raging torrent to save the drowning child simply because we sense that we ought to do it.

And that describes the case of John Rabe. He could have listed many reasons to justify fleeing Nanjing, including the risk to his life, his obligations to his family, and the role he could have had in the West sounding the alarm on unfolding Japanese atrocities. And given these reasons, nobody would have condemned him for this reasonable retreat.

But in the crisis moment, none of that mattered. Instead, Rabe perceived that he had an obligation, and I'd say a calling, to stand with the oppressed, and this conclusion simply blew his calculus away, even to the point of nullifying his powerful drive for self-preservation. The time for reasoning was done, the time for action had come. And, by acting on that call, he joined the inspiring ranks of the moral hero.

Moral obligation and moral calling constitute two crucial (and overlapping) dimensions to the moral life. Moral obligation is a general call to all moral agents to undertake morally good actions and refrain from morally evil actions. And moral calling, so it seems to me, is a specific obligation given to a particular individual in the form of a call for that individual to undertake a moral action not given to others in the same context. In this way, Rabe sensed a call to stay with the oppressed while other expatriates could flee while violating no obligation or call.

Obligation and call are not reducible to mere rational reflection or good desires, and we each need to explain their origin and nature. I understand both obligation and call to be borne of the call of God upon created moral agents like us to live in accord with the moral good.

Justin: But Randal, I agree at least in part. The desire to put others ahead of oneself is a desire we all have very strong reasons to promote and encourage in others—it is a good desire. Your moral hero did that moral action because of the kinds of desires he had—because of the kind of person he had become. No external call was necessary.

Sure, the initial evaluation of desires is deliberative, but that is a separate issue from the fact that, once a person possesses and is thereby motivated by good desires, they will do the morally obligatory act because it is what they will naturally want to do.

Randal: First, as I've said, I deny that the foundation of moral reasoning is deliberative in the sense you've described. Rather, we *begin* with an innate perceptual ability to grasp moral good and moral evil, and we reason from there. Moral reasoning is dependent on these axiomatic starting points.

As for Rabe, it isn't merely that he had good desires and acted on them. Rather, he sensed an obligation particular to him to stay behind in solidarity with the oppressed. As I've said, this sense of specific *obligation* seems to be a form of *calling*. And callings like this are not merely generated internally as we reflect on our own individual desires. Rather, they transcend the moral agent and impose restrictions upon our moral action.

Ethicist C. Stephen Evans provides a good description of moral obligations, noting that they "involve a kind of verdict on an action, they make it possible to bring reflection on action to closure and make a decision about the action by providing a decisive reason for action, they are the kinds of things people are rightly held responsible for doing or omitting, and they hold for human persons just as human persons."[5]

And, as I've said, I would add that specific obligations placed on individuals in particular contexts are best understood as particular moral callings. The challenge of any theory of ethics is to explain the force and binding nature of these moral obligations.

As a theist, this dimension of the moral life makes good sense to me, since I believe moral obligations and callings are constituted by God's commands to his creatures to act in accord with moral value in specific situations. In the case of Nanjing's refugee crisis, Rabe sensed the divine command that was perceived as a binding obligation to remain behind with the refugees.

Justin: Well, I don't deny that there are strong emotional forces pulling us to and from different actions in our moral decision-making. I just think this is explained by the complexity and potency that is the internal struggle of desires—the only reasons for action that actually exist. Sometimes the answer of what we should do is utterly obvious and, at other times, it isn't.

Randal: Thanks Justin; that's a candid response. So it would seem that, on your view, that sense of transcendent moral calling that John Rabe experienced to remain behind with and defend the oppressed was nothing more than a subjective emotion in response to his internal desires.

Justin: Nothing more than subjective emotion? What you view as transcendent, I recognize as the internal battle between desires we must all struggle with. Some of us are better at it than others. Morality, like many other aspects of life, takes practice.

Randal: But by taking that position you've *eviscerated* moral obligation of its binding force. Let's say that Bruce is studying to be a plastic surgeon and his plan is to have a career doing cosmetic surgery for rich women in Beverly Hills. Suddenly he senses a call to change his life course completely and instead devote his career to healing poverty-stricken war refugees in sub-Saharan Africa. On your view, what Bruce interprets as a binding, transcendent call of selfless service is really nothing more than Bruce's own reflections on his internal desires. But once you say that, the call loses its transcendent, binding force. You might as well say, "Bruce, it's all in your head!"

Justin: Rhetoric aside, I don't think this is a problem in the least. I think it's simply recognizing that desires are what motivate us. For you, it's a desire to please God. Inescapably though, a desire *is* what motivates your action. And, whether we like it or not, the brain that gives rise to those desires, even if that isn't the full picture, is found *in your head.*

Randal: Obviously we both think moral values and obligations are in our heads in the sense that we grasp them with our brains. But you've provided no *account* of moral obligation beyond your internal subjective desires. By contrast, on my view, John Rabe and Bruce the doctor experienced an objective, binding moral obligation, a calling from God to undertake particular heroic actions in serving the poor and destitute in accord with moral virtue. So while your account undermines the objective, unilateral binding force of moral obligation, my account explains it.

Justin: I've never once claimed that moral obligation simply boils down to my subjective desires. I've consistently claimed that morally obligatory acts are acts that persons with good desires would do in that situation. Moral obligation is about important kinds of desires. Now, if you don't mind, I have a question I'd like to ask about this moral perception of yours before we move on.

Randal: Then ask it! You don't need my permission.

COULD GOD COMMAND SOMETHING MORALLY HEINOUS?

Justin: Admittedly, the following question deals with a specific theistic tradition (rather than mere classical theism as we've been so far discussing), but I think it might be useful in understanding how this perception functions on your view. We are both quite familiar with the story of the binding of Isaac. If you were there, would you have *directly perceived* what Abraham was willing to do as an evil act?

Randal: No problem, that's fair game. Even if our primary focus is classical theism, I have made particular references to Christian theism in particular, and of course I *am* a Christian, so it is legitimate for you to ask about a specific part of the biblical narrative.

Justin: I knew it!

Randal: Let me first say that Jews and Christians have always taken a range of views over how to *interpret* narratives like the Akedah (the binding of Isaac), which is referenced in Genesis 22. Some interpreters have taken this to be a historical event that happened in the past. But others have interpreted it as a nonhistorical, allegorical tale with theological significance. Others believe it is historical, but they insist that a range of textual cues support the reading that Abraham knew God was not really demanding sacrifice. Still others adopt a sort of hybrid view, by taking the story in the terms of what Karl Barth called *saga*, which Barth views as something like an allegorical tale with some shadowy historical antecedent. My point is that interpretation of this narrative is an *intramural debate* among Jews and Christians. And the debate over how to interpret Genesis 22 does not affect my tradition of Christianity, let alone theism simpliciter.

With that long preamble out of the way, let me take the bull by the horns and address your question directly. What would *I* do if I believed God was telling me to kill my child as a spiritual sacrifice?

Simple. I'd seek counselling and medical advice. I'm guessing you would as well. I hope that response isn't too disappointing, but it's the truth. If I came to believe God was calling me to kill my child, I'd believe it was more likely that I was delusional than that God was calling me to kill my child, and I'd act accordingly.

Justin: Well, for your sake and for the sake of your child, I'm glad to hear it.

Perhaps you can help my confusion. In the context of an earlier argument, you've remarked about the *epistemic* distance that exists between our knowledge of the moral realm and God's knowledge of the moral realm. After all, if God is omniscient, she will know all possible goods and evils that could possibly exist and how they relate.

If that's true, and if God has a morally sufficient reason beyond your finite, human understanding for commanding what you believe her to be commanding, then you shouldn't expect to know what that justifying reason is, correct?

Randal: Um, yeah, sure. If God commands *p*, I shouldn't expect to know why God commands *p*. By analogy, if the master mechanic working on my car asks me to hand him the cobalt screw extractor set, I shouldn't expect to know *why* he has asked me to hand him the cobalt screw extractor set. But I can still ask whether he *has* asked me to hand him the cobalt screw extractor set. (After all, I could be wrong about *that*.)

As a Christian, I believe God rejects what is commonly called *redemptive violence*—that is, the use of violent means to bring about reconciliation between alienated parties. I believe the death of Jesus brings an end to all such appeals to violence as a means of reconciliation. As a result, I will have a strong defeater to any claim that God is now commanding violence as a means of reconciliation. And that certainly encompasses the most sacred bond of the parent/child relationship.

So, as a Christian, I will have a strong reason to reject as genuine any perceived call of God to wreak violence upon my beloved progeny.

Justin: Okay, but I'm not entirely sure that is relevant in this case. After all, as you've suggested, God's omniscience doesn't merely entail that there are *some* moral truths beyond our grasp. It also suggests that you are in no position to say that this one reason you've identified is even loosely representative of the total reasons that God has available to her for acting. Moreover, we could, for the sake of the thought experiment, bring you back in time and place you in Abraham's shoes.

It would seem, then, that you are in no position to guess the likelihood of God commanding that of you. For all you know, God has a supremely magnificent good, which can only be achieved through this initially unfortunate event.

Randal: Sure it is *logically possible* that God could command something that appears to be morally heinous. But, for goodness sake, Justin, something parallel to that is true of *every* moral theory. Take your own theory predicated on moral desires. It's *logically possible* that moral desires could require actions that appear to be morally heinous. Since you're raising a point that applies trivially to every moral system, I fail to see what you hope to accomplish by pushing that particular issue on me.

Justin: I worry you've missed the more important of the two points, Randal. Notice that I'm not *just* saying that it's logically possible that God might permit something that appears to you as morally heinous. That wouldn't be terribly interesting all by itself. Rather, I've made the additional claim that, given the epistemic distance between you and God, you are in no position to place likelihoods either way. That second part deserves some serious focus.

Randal: On the contrary, the cases are parallel on that point too. How do you know that you are not in a precisely parallel situation regarding *your* epistemic distance from the right moral desires? In other words, how do you know that the right moral desires are not ones you now consider morally heinous?

Justin: Of course it's possible that I am wrong about a particular obligation I believe I have or don't have. As you pointed out, that's a potential issue on all views. Besides, that's not even what I'm pressing here.

You've said that, if you were to start thinking God was commanding you to do something you directly perceived as heinous (like killing your child or torturing and killing a POW, which you earlier said was always wrong no matter the circumstances), you would think yourself more likely delusional than that God was *really* commanding that act.

Randal: Yup.

Justin: However, this reaction to my hypothetical shows that you believe yourself to have sufficient representative knowledge of the reasons God has available to her in order to claim that God *probably* would never command such a thing. Would you agree?

Randal: I'm glad you're conceding that *every* moral theory faces the same hypothetical that a person could be radically incorrect in their current moral beliefs, whether those beliefs concern moral obligations, moral values, or desires. But I'm surprised that you don't see how that fact undermines your whole line of questioning.

As for my current moral beliefs, as I said, a person's fundamental knowledge of moral value on which moral obligations are predicated is not arrived at discursively by grasping particular reasons for action and inferring moral values and obligations from them. Rather, they are perceived immediately, as with Tolstoy's immediate perception of the evil of capital punishment.

Justin: Yes, I'm aware that this is your view. My question though is not about *how* you perceive moral facts. Rather, my question is about *how much* is being perceived.

Now, I'm sure we can agree that, given that God is morally perfect, God would not command something unless she had a morally sufficient reason to do so. It follows then that, when you responded to my hypothetical scenario about coming to believe that God was commanding you to kill your child by saying,

"I'd believe it was more likely that I was delusional than that God was calling me to kill my child."

we can translate that to,

"I'd believe it was more likely that I was delusional than that God has a morally sufficient reason to command me to kill my child."

Now, as finite beings, we might not be able to perceive any morally sufficient reason at all why an omniscient God, if she exists, would command such a killing or any other instance of evil for that matter. But the question *I've* been trying to get at is, does it logically follow that, just because we cannot perceive such a morally justifying reason for God to command you to kill your child, that it is therefore *more likely* that you are delusional?

Randal: But Justin, *I'm not a utilitarian.* In other words, I believe there are all sorts of actions that I could never have a moral obligation or moral calling to perform. For example, as I've already said, I believe torture and rape are *categorically evil.* Since I believe those actions are necessarily immoral, it follows that I could never have a moral obligation to torture or rape another person. I have the same view about devotional child killing, and I've defended that view in a conference paper called "I want to give the baby to God: Three theses on devotional child killing."[6]

Justin: Well, color me confused. On the one hand, you claim that certain acts are *necessarily immoral.* And yet, earlier you said that *it is merely more likely* that you are delusional than that God wants you to kill your child.

If you think that God commanding you to kill your child is not impossible, then how were you able to entertain my hypothetical in the first place? We could have saved some time if you had just argued my hypothetical was incoherent in the first place.

Randal, you've said you're not a utilitarian. I wonder though, do you think God is? For example, in the previous discussion on religious disagreement, you suggest that God allows certain horrific evils to occur in the world for some greater good.

Randal: Unfortunately you keep trying to hammer a point that I've already responded to. But let me restate my reply a bit differently.

First, as I said, I believe there are a range of actions that are categorically immoral, and, as such, they could never be morally permissible to perform, including rape, torture, cannibalism, devotional child killing, and so on. Since these are categorically immoral, no divine being would ever *command* them.

Ahh, you say, but what if God *did* command them? What then? Huh? Huh?

And this brings me back to the second point I've already made. While you seem to think that these *per impossibile* scenarios that you keep raising present a unique problem for theism, the reality is that *the exact same scenarios can be presented to the atheist ethicist like yourself.*

For example, at present you agree with me that the desires to perform actions like rape, torture, cannibalism, and devotional child killing are categorically immoral. But what if you come to believe that the morally right desire *is* to rape, torture, cannibalize, and kill? Then you'll need to rape, torture, cannibalize, and kill!

Justin: My confusion here was flowing from the fact that you were entertaining my hypothetical in a way that seemed you merely thought it less likely that God would command such a thing rather than flat-out impossible.

That said, you raise a good point. If I were to fall under the radical delusion of thinking that the desire to rape or torture are the kinds of desires that, when introduced or increased, tend to fulfill desires rather than thwart them, and that therefore rape or torture could, in certain circumstances, become obligatory, I'd also seek help from a mental health professional.

Randal: Well, we can certainly high five on that point!

MORAL KNOWLEDGE AND SKEPTICISM

Randal: But since you've returned us to the topic of moral epistemology, I think this is an important question for *you* to address. I'm interested to hear more about your defense of moral knowledge on atheism.

Perhaps the most well-known atheist of the twentieth century, Bertrand Russell, famously described the position of the atheist as follows: "A strange mystery it is that nature, omnipotent but blind, in the revolutions of her secular hurryings through the abysses of space, has brought forth at last a child, subject still to her power, but gifted with sight, with knowledge of good and evil, with the capacity of judging all the works of his unthinking mother."[7]

I agree with Russell: that is a strange mystery indeed. As nature cycles along, she produces creatures that are adapted for *survival*, not *truth*. But once we adopt the atheistic view that we were formed to acquire adaptive beliefs rather than true beliefs, we face a daunting skeptical problem: how do we know our adaptive beliefs *are* true? Richard Rorty (himself an atheist) put it like this: "The idea that one species of organism is unlike all the others, oriented not just toward its own increated prosperity but toward Truth, is as un-Darwinian as the idea that every human being has a built-in moral compass—a conscience that swings free of both social history and individual luck."[8]

Rorty is right. Blind nature produces creatures oriented toward their increased prosperity, not toward truth. And that brings me to my question: what is *your basis* for thinking that your desires track moral facts successfully, that they yield genuine moral *knowledge*?

Justin: It is not my position that mere desires track moral truth. There is a big difference between, say, holding that whatever I desire is what is good and what I've advocated above. Recall that desires, because they are the only reasons for action that exist, are properly the primary objects of evaluation.

We can evaluate desires by their tendency to fulfill or thwart other desires. Some tend to fulfill and some tend to thwart. Good actions are those actions that persons with good desires relevant to that situation would do. So, the primary question in morality involves the tendency of certain desires to fulfill or thwart other desires. That is an empirical issue. There is nothing in principle preventing us from evaluating them as to their relation to other desires. Admittedly, some of those questions will be much easier to answer than others.

Now, if your question is about blind nature and its implications on our beliefs *in general*, which is what you seem to be hinting at, that seems to me like a much broader question beyond the scope of this particular chapter.

Randal: As I have explained, as a theist I believe that God equipped human beings with a faculty of moral perception that enables us to attain moral knowledge about the world. Like sense perception and rational intuition, moral perception is not infallible, but *it is directed at truth* because God wants us to attain moral knowledge about the world as surely as he wants us to gain sense perceptual and rational knowledge.

In short, if we were created by a God who desires us to gain moral knowledge, then it is highly likely that our moral faculties would produce moral knowledge. As a result, just as I am prima facie justified in accepting the deliverances of sense perception and rational intuition, so I am prima facie justified in accepting the deliverances of moral perception.

By contrast, as an atheist you believe our cognitive faculties (moral faculties included) evolved gradually, spurred on by selective pressures that were *directed not to truth, but to adaptive value.* Given that your cognitive faculties are oriented toward adaptation rather than truth, what basis do you have for believing they do produce truth?

Justin: Well, because the kinds of cognitive faculties that selective pressures directed at adaptive value would likely bring about would also be the kinds of cognitive faculties that are generally reliable at tracking truth.

Randal: That sounds circular to me. Justin, what *reason* do you have to believe selective pressures are largely truth conducive? After all, I can provide plenty of counterexamples.

Consider the example of clinical psychopaths. These are people who appear to lack the moral perceptual abilities that I've said are the possession of properly functioning human beings. And yet, as Paul Babiak and Robert Hare point out in their book *Snakes in Suits: When Psychopaths Go to Work*, psychopaths flourish in certain social environments.[9] They are disproportionately represented among successful Wall Street stock traders and corporate CEOs, for example.

But if psychopaths can flourish despite having a dysfunctional moral perception, how do you know that all of us are not likewise radically deficient when it comes to grasping moral facts? As I said, what justifies the claim?

Justin: Sorry, it's just not clear to me how this is supposed to be an objection to what I've said here. You seem to want to attribute to me the claim that an improperly functioning cognitive faculty in a person could never be compatible with that person flourishing in some *specific* role in modern life. I have not made any such claim.

If it were not the case that the belief-forming mechanisms we've evolved were generally reliable, then we are without a remotely plausible explanation of important bits of background knowledge, such as our long-term survival in a wide variety of changing environments. The claim that our belief-forming cognitive faculties are generally reliable is a much better explanation for this fact than the claim that they are generally unreliable.

Randal: I plead innocent of the charge! I didn't attribute that claim to you. My point is this: your view that our moral perception was formed for adaptive value rather than to gain truth undermines your justification for accepting the deliverances of our moral perception *as true*. The case of psychopaths—that is, individuals who can flourish while having moral perception radically different from that of the general population—merely illustrates my point.

You and I agree that our cognitive faculties, including our moral perception, are generally *reliable*. But reliable *for what?* I believe they are reliable for gaining *true beliefs*. The most you can say is that they are reliable for attaining *adaptive* beliefs. That's a big difference.

In short, your account of moral perception provides an undercutting defeater to the deliverances of moral perception. An atheistic view of the origin of moral perception undermines the deliverances of moral perception.

Justin: Randal, thanks for spelling that out more. Your distinction between cognitive faculties being reliably adaptive and reliably delivering true beliefs is a good one.

Randal: Awesome! So I'm right! Why don't we call it a day and celebrate? The drinks are on me!

Justin: Unfortunately, this argument is a complete non-sequitur.

Randal: Waiter, cancel my drink order!

Justin: Oh, by all means, I'll still have the drink.

Randal: Okay, waiter, I'll have a pint of your finest strong barley wine in a crystal goblet. And you can give my friend something colorful in a fancy glass with a cocktail umbrella.

So now, where were we?

Justin: My concern here is that your conclusion that my justification for accepting the deliverances of any belief-forming cognitive process (moral perception or any other) as true is in any way undermined does not logically follow from the claim that these processes were evolved primarily for their *adaptive* value.

Perhaps you've oversimplified the issue and forgotten an important premise regarding the relationship between a belief-forming mechanism being adaptive and its deliverances being reliably true.

Randal: Sorry Justin, but I must disagree with you here. And I need to exonerate myself of your charge. My memory's not perfect, but I didn't forget any premises. The fact is that you need to *defend* the premise that adaptive moral beliefs are likely to be *true*, for that's the very claim I'm challenging. Until you defend that premise, you are only justified in believing your moral perception is adaptive, not that it is truth conducive. And thus it follows that you rationally ought to withhold assent to the deliverances of your moral perception because *you have no basis to believe they are likely to be true.*

Justin: While this specific argument is taking place at the tail end of a discussion of morality, I do not think it necessary that we continue to limit ourselves to talking merely about moral perception and moral beliefs. The argument you're attempting to run here is clearly much broader in scope. It's an argument about belief-forming cognitive faculties in general.

Randal: While you could apply this kind of argument to reason generally, I've intentionally focused here on morality.

Justin: Before I defend my statement above, I think it might be useful for the both of us to back up and get clear on what's being said. Maybe I've completely missed the boat here.

Randal: Okay, I'll return to the dock. I wouldn't want you to miss the boat and be left to quaff your fancy cocktail all alone.

Justin: Now, on a common atheistic view, beliefs are neurological structures that have at least neurophysiological properties and semantic properties/content (There is a cliff up ahead; the sky is blue; there is water to my left).

Randal: Proceed with caution, Justin. The claim that beliefs just are neurological structures is a highly controversial view in the philosophy of mind. Regardless, it isn't an *atheistic* view, since atheism and theism completely underdetermine theories of mind. In other words, a theist could accept your identity claim and an atheist could reject it.

Justin: Ah, yes. You are correct about that.

Randal: Fortunately, my argument does not at all depend on any particular theory of mind.

Justin: If I understand you correctly, your worry, in part, is that what matters from an unguided evolutionary perspective is simply the behavior of an organism. Unguided evolution doesn't care whether the beliefs causally associated with any particular action have content (semantic) that is actually true about the world. It is assumed in the argument that, unlike the potentially causal physiological properties of a belief, the *content* of a belief is causally irrelevant and so hidden—in a functional sense at least—from the selective pressures of unguided evolution. Am I being fair to your argument so far?

Randal: I wouldn't say it is necessarily hidden, but it is in inadequate to ground more than merely adaptive belief. In other words, unguided evolution can secure beliefs that are adaptive, but that doesn't cash out to beliefs that are *true*. At the risk of repeating myself, let me go ahead and repeat myself.

Justin: If you insist. I'm just trying to get clear on the argument.

Randal: As I already said, you need to defend the premise that adaptive moral beliefs are likely to be *true*. Until you defend that premise, you are only justified in believing that your moral beliefs are adaptive, not that they are true. Until you defend that premise, your only reasonable response is moral skepticism.

Justin: Okay, okay, okay. Hold onto your britches.

Randal: Is that what you call these? Britches? And all this time I thought they were lederhosen! Barley wine tastes better when you're wearing lederhosen.

Justin: Let me now explain *why* atheists are within their epistemic rights to accept that their cognitive belief-forming faculties, which have evolved for adaptive reasons, will also reliably track true beliefs.

Randal: Awesome! Do tell. The suspense is killing me!

Justin: Suppose that I took a walk in an unfamiliar wooded area that happens to be filled with hungry tigers. There are certainly possible scenarios in which I survive these walks by having false beliefs. For example, it's possible that beliefs like "This forest is filled with beautiful women dressed in convincing tiger cosplay" and "Beautiful women engaged in tiger cosplay take their roles seriously and will attack and kill me if I'm noticed" may get me through unscathed.

But, when we consider the total number of possible false beliefs that I could have had about the situation, it seems clear that only a small minority of false beliefs will just happen to be of the sort that manage to put me through the forest populated with hungry tigers alive. The subset of false beliefs that specifically and systematically recommend the kind of necessary avoidance behavior are a relatively small subset of the total number of false beliefs that it was possible for me to have. So, while it is certainly possible to identify false beliefs with which I could survive a forest of hungry tigers, I am far more likely to survive that forest if the majority of my beliefs about my surroundings are true rather than false.[10]

Randal: To summarize the essence of your response, shorn of the fanciful, feminine, feline fluff, it seems that you're simply stating that it "seems clear" to you "that only a small minority of false beliefs" will be adaptive and false. But, as I pointed out with the case of cognitively deficient but flourishing psychopaths, that *isn't* clear, not at all.

Justin: But, Randal, that it seems clear to me wasn't the only thing I've said on the matter. As a conceptual exercise, consider the total number of logically possible false beliefs. Now, take that total and compare it to the subset that is the total number of logically possible false beliefs that reliably encourage behavior that is generally adaptive in a broad number of circumstances. Given that this is a very *specific condition*, only a minority of false beliefs will actually meet it.

Randal: To switch from tigers back to morality, as I said I pointed to real cases of individuals like psychopaths, who flourish despite having a moral perception radically different from ours. The fact is that you simply haven't shown that atheism is likely to secure moral perception that reliably tracks objective moral facts. Consequently, as I said, the consistent atheist position regarding moral perception is *skepticism*. And giving up moral knowledge is a high cost for atheism.

Of course, there is a silver lining to this dark cloud. If you believe you have reliable moral knowledge, then you should be a theist!

But, once again, I suspect we are not going to agree on this! So it's probably time to move onto another topic. Any ideas?

Justin: I've argued that, although our belief-forming cognitive faculties evolved to be adaptive, this shouldn't worry us about the reliability of those faculties for producing true beliefs. This is because, as I've argued above, true beliefs, moral or mundane, are more likely to be adaptive than false beliefs. As a result, the consequence of skepticism, moral or otherwise, that you've attempted to burden atheists with doesn't stick. To be clear, there may be reasons that could be offered in support of moral skepticism, but this isn't one of them.

Randal: I feel sick that my slick shtick doesn't stick.

Justin: I also worry that your defense of theism's ability to provide moral knowledge is problematic, but I think that discussion will be a better fit for a *later* chapter we've got planned, on arguments that appeal to facts about suffering in our world.

Randal: Okey-dokey. Thanks for the heads up!

So time to move on then?

Justin: Yeah, that's enough of that I suppose. If you're looking for other topic ideas, I've got a different argument I'd like to bounce off of you. I think it's a decent argument, but I must admit that I haven't had many critical eyes on it just yet. Maybe you'll convince me otherwise.

Randal: I'll do my best!

Chapter 5

THE PROBLEM OF THE HOSTILITY OF THE UNIVERSE

Justin: I suppose the best way for me to begin unpacking this argument would be to provide an illustration of sorts.

Randal: Sounds good. Vivid illustrations are a great way to, er, illustrate things. What sort were you thinking of?

A MOST UNUSUAL BIRTHDAY GIFT

Justin: How about this? Imagine an extraordinarily wealthy businessman who, for transparently aptronymic purposes, shall be named Rich. For all intents and purposes, Rich has limitless financial resources. Let's also imagine that our wealthy mogul is a father and has designed and overseen the building of an immense skyscraper for his son, Adam. That building, while serving perhaps unknown secondary purposes, exists primarily to be a residence for Adam.

Randal: Okay, so rich Mr. Rich built a tower primarily for his son, Adam. Adam's Tower. Got it.

Justin: Prior to being handed the keys to the massive entryway on his eighteenth birthday, Adam had never seen the inside of the massive and ornate construction.

Randal: Wow, that definitely beats my eighteenth birthday! I know what Adam's probably thinking: *house party*!

Justin: Ah, well not so fast.

See, upon entering the homestead for the first time, he realizes that the building is entirely hollow, like a towering grain silo. The only floor is the ground floor. There are no elevators, no ladders, and yet the towering walls and ceiling are artistic masterpieces of incredible detail. So, while gorgeous to behold, the rest of the building seems mightily superfluous.

Now, let's say that there is some shelving such that, if Adam was sufficiently careful, could be climbed. So, he starts climbing, because why not?

Randal: I totally get that. I love climbing shelves too.

Justin: Unfortunately for Adam, he quickly realizes that the air, starting at just ten feet, is unbreathable. Some unknown gas hovers there and extends all the way to the ceiling. The building is positively dangerous for anybody without their feet firmly on the ground.

Randal: Goodness me, that's a strange gift.

Justin: It's a *very* strange gift.

Randal: Yeah, a *very VERY* strange gift! (Sorry, I couldn't resist.)

Justin: Given that I'm just making stuff up for analogy purposes, let me make the story even more interesting and relevant to the topic of the book. Let's say that, prior to receiving the keys to his new home, Adam was accidentally struck in the head and lost all memory of his past interactions with his father.

Randal: Ouch, that's gotta hurt. Even better, let's say Adam was hit in the head by the last remaining piece of Skylab.

Justin: Without these important memories, Adam has no past experience of his own from which he can get a sense of his father's moral character. His father's moral character is completely ambiguous.

So, after that absurd story-telling session, one interesting question comes to mind. After entering the house and discovering the dangerous design plan, should Adam conclude that his father is loving or indifferent?

Randal: Well, if I were Adam, I'd definitely be perplexed.

Justin: Same here.

Randal: In particular, I'd wonder if dear old dad really made this building just for me or whether he made it for some greater purpose of which I was a part. It certainly would seem rather curious to assume that it was made just for me in light of what you've said. Especially the bit about the deadly gas!

Justin: Hmm. Interesting point. Could you give an example of what you mean by that? I can certainly understand the idea of building something for multiple reasons, but what plausible end could be served by the noxious gas?

Randal: That's my point. It *doesn't* make sense. If I were Adam, I don't know that I would be in a place to know what the point of the poisonous gas is. All I would know is that *it presumably isn't there for me to breathe.*

Justin: You don't think you should be in a place to know the point of the gas? If your father built the home and gave you the keys to move in, you don't think you'd be entitled to an explanation of the poisonous gas? You don't think you'd be within your epistemic rights to be *surprised* by the gas if we were to start with the assumption that the father is a loving one?

Randal: Sure, you can be surprised all you like. As I said, it would be reasonable at that point to *question* whether the building was, in fact, made for me. But I don't want to get on a tangent. Why don't I close my yap and finish my barley wine while you unpack the rest of your illustration and the argument that goes with it?

Justin: I think it's certainly fair to accept that the building probably has other purposes besides serving as your residence. The question is one about whether or not we'd be told what the purpose was and warned of potential dangers to our person.

But, yes, you're right. I should probably get on to presenting the argument in a way that explicitly touches on those issues.

I'm sure it's no surprise that the story is an attempt at an analogy. The skyscraper is our universe, Adam is us, and the father is a God character. In the story, the question of interest is whether or not certain design features of the home are suggestive about the moral character of the father. Of course, if we shift from the analogy to talking about the universe and God, we are going to be asking whether or not certain features of the universe are suggestive of the very existence of a God for which moral perfection is an essential attribute.

Randal: Ah, I see things coming into focus. Can you unpack it further?

Justin: The argument begins with a pretty well-known fact.

Near Universal Hostility: The vast majority of our universe is hostile[1] to most forms of biological life we know of.

In his book *Death from the Skies*, astronomer Philip Plait writes,

The Universe is an incredibly hostile place for life. Virtually all of it is a vacuum, so that's bad right from the start. Of the extremely few places that aren't hard vacuum, most are too hot for chemical reactions to do very well—molecules get blasted apart before they can even properly form. Of the places that aren't too hot, most are too cold—reactions happen too slowly to get interesting things to occur in the first place.[2]

I want to argue that atheism leads us to expect near universal hostility toward most life more than does theism.[3]

Randal: So *that's* what this is all about! Atheism, eh?! I should have seen that coming!

Justin: Yes, sir.

Randal: Okay, now bring the point home while I map out my amazing rebuttal with this piece of sidewalk chalk.

Justin: So, Randal, one reason why this fact about near universal hostility is more expected on atheism than it is on theism is that theism gives us some reasons that atheism does not to expect that the universe was created, at least in part, with life in mind. On theism then, we have *some* reasons at least to expect features of the universe not to be hostile to life. Any number of reasons not to expect the near universal hostility toward most life will be more reasons than atheism has.

Randal: Makes sense; I can see where you're coming from.

Justin: Secondly, on atheism we have strong reasons to expect near universal hostility toward most of life in this way. Given that there are many more ways for a universe to be, in general, hostile to life than for a universe to be, in general, friendly to life, generally hostile universes make up a much larger slice of possibility pie than do friendly universes. It is more likely, then, that life-friendly conditions are much more likely to fall onto the larger, hostile slice of the possibility pie.

Randal: Possibility pie? Mmm, sounds tasty!

But before going any further, can't you raise the same supposed objection about planet earth that you raise about the universe in general? After all, most of planet earth is hostile to human life, including oceans, frozen wasteland, scorching desert, and various other inhospitable environments.

Justin: Yes, one could certainly do that. The earth also has many features that I would argue are better explained on an atheistic universe than on a universe created by a maximally loving God. But I think it's useful to distinguish between those facts that hold locally and that pose problems of natural suffering (a phrase used to describe suffering that is not the result of human-free decisions) and those that are broader in scope.

The problem of hostility garners part of its strength by observing that the universe is so profoundly large. Our observable universe is roughly 93 billion light years from end to end.

If we conservatively assume, then, that just our observable universe is what exists, then the proportion of life-friendly parts to life-averse parts is just, well, astronomical.

Randal: Pun intended?!

Justin: *Bows*

Randal: Ahh, I see. Your puns are truly out of this world. That deserves the slow clap!

Justin: Now, when we fully appreciate the size of just our observable universe, we appear to be profoundly insignificant from a cosmic perspective. On theism, this hostile to friendly proportion is not at all what we would expect.

Randal: I agree that we seem pretty insignificant. But as for your claim that we wouldn't expect a "hostile to friendly proportion" on theism, where'd that come from? So you think if there is a God he would have ensured the universe is full of breathable air and heated to a balmy seventy degrees? Sorry, but I don't follow your logic here.

Justin: I'm certainly not claiming that if there was a God, she would make things maximally comfortable. That said, there is nothing unreasonable about expecting an environment created by a maximally loving being for her created creatures to be less of a death trap than it actually is. After all, Philip Plait observes, "In reality, the Universe cares not at all if we live or die. If a human were magically transported to any random spot in the cosmos, within seconds he'd die 99.999999999999 percent of the time. At best."[4]

Expecting the universe not to be so thoroughly deadly isn't the same as expecting the universe to be a day spa, though that would be pretty nice too!

Randal: A cosmic day spa. That'd certainly give new meaning to the "Whirlpool Galaxy"! Har har har.

But seriously, I'm still not buying your logic here.

Justin: If I was to put it another way, suppose we were to come across a car almost completely covered in dirt and grime, inside and out, and filled with trash. A thoroughly filthy car, except for one small and perfectly clean spot on the driver-side door. Given that information, there are some claims that are more reasonable to make about its owner than others. For example, supposing that Mr. Clean owns and maintains the car is not a particularly reasonable conclusion to arrive at given the information available to us.

Randal: Like you, I would expect a good car owner to keep his car clean, all the more so if he went under the moniker "Mr. Clean." But I don't think that a dirty car is a relevant analogy to a universe that is generally hostile to sentient life.

Perhaps we should pause for a minute to remember the definition of God that we're working with. As we agreed, God is a necessarily existent person who is omniscient, omnipotent, and perfectly good. Note that our definition does *not* require that God would be likely to make the universe (or planet earth) maximally or even generally hospitable for human creatures or other sentient life.

Justin: Well, I sure *hope* that my argument doesn't suggest I've forgotten the definition of God we've agreed upon for this conversation.

Randal: I'm not so sure. It seems to me that your argument is an objection not to theism simpliciter but rather to *anthropocentrism* (i.e., the view that the universe was created for human beings). Indeed, you stated this quite explicitly in your initial illustration of a man named Rich who builds a tower *for his son, Adam,* and then hands over the keys on his birthday. But theism does not entail anthropocentrism. No theist need think God created the universe just for human beings.

Nor for that matter, is *Christian* theism committed to anthropocentrism. For example, one standard view within Christian theology is that God created the universe *for his own glory.* A mind-numbingly large universe that is almost completely hostile to sentient life may not serve *our* immediate interests, but that's quite different from claiming it doesn't serve God's. So it seems to me your argument is wide of the mark.

THEISM, ANTHROPOCENTRISM, AND A BATTLE OF ANALOGIES

Justin: Hold up, Randal. I think it's vitally important to bring attention to the fact that, in unpacking my initial illustration, I claimed that the skyscraper may serve *multiple* purposes—not just that of being a residence for Adam. That aspect of the analogy is consistent with the fact that, on theism, the universe could serve many of God's purposes, of which being a residence for humans was one. Indeed, I've never sought to saddle you or any other theist with the anthropocentric claim that the universe was created solely for human beings.

That said, human beings do exist *within* the universe and that is relevant background knowledge.

Randal: Indeed, we do. And indeed, that is.

Justin: And so, if theism is true, God has created human beings in the universe. Clearly then, at least one of the purposes of the universe is to serve as a residence for created beings.

Human enjoyment, flourishing, or even survival in the universe may not be the primary goal behind God's act of creation of the universe, but that is neither here nor there, because we've stipulated that God is morally perfect. Consider some other goal plausibly consistent with God's moral perfection that may be behind the creation of any universe. Suggesting that such a goal—whatever it may be—could not be attained by an omnipotent being without God creating 99.99 percent of the universe to be a death trap to moral agents is to make profoundly unimpressive the concept of omnipotence.

If you recently heard of the poisonous gas permanently hovering ten feet above the ground floor in Adam's new skyscraper house, I presume that accusations of Adam-centric reasoning wouldn't distract you much from your justified suspicions about Adam's father—the designer and architect with limitless resources.

Randal: I still think your analogy is flawed. The universe just isn't analogous to a skyscraper house for human beings to reside in, and it is no part of theism to think it is. Nor, as I said, does Christianity entail or even suggest that God created the universe to be the home of our particular species. That's a deeply misleading metaphor.

Here's a different analogy, one that I think is more accurate and thus less apt to mislead. On this scenario, Rich creates a safe, warm bungalow for his son, Adam, at the top of a cliff overlooking a stormy sea. From the porch of his bungalow, Adam can take in the breathtaking spectacle far below: dark, heaving swells crashing into rocks, howling gales of chill wind, and even the occasional awe-inspiring iceberg. From the windows of the warm, safe bungalow (i.e., his home), Adam can witness the austere endless expanses of the beautiful yet hostile ocean.

Justin: Admittedly, that analogy is slightly prettier than my poison-gas-filled skyscraper.

Randal: Definitely. And I didn't even mention the crackling fire, lilting smooth jazz playing on the stereo, and Adam's glass of hot buttered rum.

Justin: Stop trying to seduce me, Randal.

Randal: Er, okay, this is awkward.

Now, moving along, in this scenario it's quite clear that Rich did not fashion the ocean, cliffs, and rocky shore to serve as Adam's home. Rather, the young man's home is the bungalow, a lovely, safe retreat from the dangerous, severe, and yet glorious landscape. And that's a fitting analogue for our home here on planet earth. We have a unique, glorious vantage point on the austere beauty and majesty of the universe all around us, a vantage point that comes into view shortly after every sunset. But make no mistake: while Adam's home is by the sea, the sea itself was never meant to be Adam's home. And while our pale blue dot is located in the vast, hostile universe, that universe beyond earth was never meant to be our home (at least not without some ambitious terraforming).

Justin: I don't understand why you keep saying the universe wasn't meant to be our home. Clearly we reside *in* the universe. I think what you mean is that only a small fraction was ever meant to be our home because it's not as though the earth is not itself a part of the universe.

Randal: Of course, I understand your point: spatially earth is located *within* the universe. But look at it this way: The man who lives on an island in the ocean does not say his home is *the ocean*. Rather, he says his home is the island that is in the ocean. In *that* sense I don't say our home is the universe. Rather, I say our home is a terrestrial island *in* the universe.

Also keep in mind either way that calling the universe our *home* is still a metaphor. And as the skyscraper illustration makes clear, it is a *misleading* metaphor. In my illustration, Adam's home is the life-friendly cabin that is located in proximity to the hostile sea. And that is a correct analogue for our life-friendly planet earth that is located in proximity to the hostile universe. In both cases, the home itself is not hostile but the environs beyond the home are.

Justin: With regard to your story, the obvious and relevant difference that pops out to me here is that, in your analogy, what is being created is one place within a larger, preexisting dangerous context (cliff, stormy sea). One of the points that the skyscraper analogy is supposed to tease out is the fact that the danger was *part of the design plan* rather than just a fact about some unfortunate context in which a home was built.

After all, theism doesn't posit a God who had no choice but to create in some preexisting dangerous space. Theism posits a God who has designed and created everything from the ground up. God was cooking from scratch.

Randal: That is indeed a difference, but I submit that it isn't a *relevant* difference for the point of analogy. All that is required for the analogy to carry is that the hostile environs (the sea, the universe) were never created with the purpose of serving as the home. But Rich *did* create a space for his son to live (the cabin) and *that* space is hospitable. And God *did* create a space for human beings to live in (planet earth) and that space is also hospitable.

Justin: Perhaps you'll find a combination of our analogies more agreeable.

In this new story, Rich uses his limitless resources to build a gigantic floating island in the middle of the ocean. Starting off this way is arguably a better fit for representing theism with most everything being designed and built intentionally. Let's also say, as in your analog, that a small bungalow was constructed for Adam. Besides that small bungalow, however, and the very small yard around it, the rest of the island is heated to extreme temperatures such that severe burns result from just touching your foot to the ground.

After being dropped off on this bizarre landmass, Adam begins exploring his new environment. Does Adam not have a right to be suspicious of his father after learning that nearly the entire island is heated to such a scalding temperature?

Randal: You forgot to mention the headhunting villagers and flying poisonous snakes. The picture you draw certainly is bizarre. But, to be honest, I don't find this multiplication of competing analogies to be helpful. On the contrary, I still find the analogy I gave far more apt (and less fanciful) to describe the actual human situation with respect to the universe, at least as I as a theist understand it.

The sea wasn't created to be Adam's home, but it is austere and awesome and beautiful just the same. And with adequate preparation and ingenuity, Adam could begin to explore it. That aptly describes our relationship to the universe as well. It is austere and awesome and beautiful, but it wasn't created for us. And with adequate preparation and ingenuity, we can begin to explore it.

But I fear we could get into a rut quibbling over which analogy is the most appropriate. Would you like to unpack the argument further in light of your chosen illustration?

WHY WOULD GOD CREATE A HOSTILE UNIVERSE?

Justin: Yes, perhaps we should set aside these analogies for now. One way to get at our core disagreement here, even if in a roundabout way, is to abstract away all the information we have and just think about theism, its conceptual contents, and what we could expect to discover about God's creative powers. If theism were true, what are some of the most plausible candidates with regard to the *reasons* why God might choose to create?

Randal: For starters, since we agree on the concept of God as perfect, this would seem to preclude God creating out of need.

Justin: Okay, that makes some sense to me. There is nothing external to herself that God requires in order to go on. God doesn't require food, water, companionship, etc.

Randal: Right, so God *doesn't* create because he's lonely and needed a friend or he's bored and needed something to do. But God can still create out of love, the love of the creation he has brought into being.

Justin: Well, okay, but shouldn't we distinguish between divine needs and divine desires? We might say that God doesn't need friends but that's not to say that she wouldn't desire to have friends. Relationships are a good thing, after all.

Randal: I suppose it depends on the relationship, but I agree that *some* relationships can be a very great good.

Justin: Okay, but what does it mean to say that God creates *out of love*? I can make no sense out of that. To my point about divine *needs* versus *wants*, people create because they find the state of affairs in which there is this new thing to be preferable to the current state of affairs. They *desire* it to be the case. Assuming the creation acts are intentional, we cannot avoid the fact that this was to fulfill God's desire for a state of affairs she found preferable. So, part of explaining why somebody did x instead of y is knowing what desires they were driven by prior to that act.

Randal: When I think of a great artist producing a work of art, I might ask a similar question: why would the artist create that painting (or sculpture or whatever)? While I may not know precisely *why*, I could at least say that it is in the artist's nature to produce great works of art like this.

Similarly, I might say that it is in God's nature to produce the creation he has produced. That may not tell us all we might *like* to know as to God's reasons for creating, but if I can't understand the mind of the artist in such matters, why should I presume to know the mind of God?

Justin: Well, artists aren't exactly silent as to their motivations for creating their works. Very often we are told that their paintings and sculptures are motivated by a deep desire for self-expression or to challenge those persons who might view it. Moreover, we can often tell something about the artist by looking at their artwork.

That said, I'm not sure it's in your best interest to say that we are without any substantive access to God's motivations.

Randal: Always looking out for my best interests! Thanks, buddy!

Justin: Just being a pal. To make that claim would be to forfeit the purpose of positing God and her creative power as a substantive *explanation* for what we observe. After all, if God exists but we can't know what God would be likely to do, how could positing God's existence purport to explain anything we actually observe?

But you said that God's creative act was out of love. Could you expound on that a bit more? What does it mean?

Randal: God is a maximally great being, and thus the acts he undertakes and the entities he brings into being (including the universe itself) are consistent with that perfect and loving nature.

Immanuel Kant famously observed, "Two things fill the mind with ever new and increasing admiration and awe, the oftener and more steadily we reflect on them: the starry heavens above me and the moral law within me."[5]

I couldn't agree more. As I was arguing earlier, I believe the moral law points to God. And I'd say the same about those starry heavens. When I contemplate the vast, majestic, and severe expanses of deep space, I am in awe of the hand of the artist and my miniscule, and yet still significant, place within this staggering scape.

Justin: Okay, so then is there anything within the concept of God and her desire to *create out of love* that would ever lead you to expect that this love-infused creation act would result in a plane of existence that is 99 percent hostile to human beings so capable of love? Moreover, how does one create something out of a love for something (or someone) that doesn't even exist *until* the point in time at which it is created?

To be clear, my argument is not asking whether our current universe is logically compatible with something a maximally great being would create. Rather it's asking how likely it is that the output of a love-inspired creation act would be so thoroughly hostile to God's created beings so capable of love.

Randal: Let's return to Adam's cozy bungalow overlooking the ocean. His father secured him a safe place to live, and that much we would expect. God, likewise, has provided us a safe planet on which to live. More specifically, he's secured a planet with safe environs for us to live in. Granted, the peaks of the Himalayas and the bottom of the sea are not that hospitable! But all of earth's various environments work together to produce a whole that is broadly hospitable to our species. As I have said, I don't see any reason to think that God would be expected to secure more than this.

But enough with my playing defense. I can also envision *good reasons* why God would place human beings within a universe that is mostly hostile to our existence. This universe provides the human species (and whatever other intelligent civilizations there may be) an extraordinary *challenge* to explore and discover. As Neil Armstrong famously observed, one small step for a man (or woman) might constitute a giant leap for the species. In short, a universe both severe and glorious offers unending possibilities for the enormous goods of human ingenuity, courage, and selflessness as we undertake discovery and exploration. And in that regard we're just getting started.

Justin: Atheism would suggest that a majority of the universe would likely not be life-friendly for the reasons I've already mentioned. On the other hand, with theism, we must address the question of God's moral nature (which you have) and God's motivating *purpose* in creating in a non-ad-hoc way. At least, that is what we must do if we are to address whether or not the kind of universe we have is to be more surprising or expected on theism than it is on atheism.

This is part of why I think it's extremely important to get much clearer on what you believe to be the reasons behind God's creation act.

Randal: And have I addressed your concerns?

Justin: I worry that I'm forced to answer this question in the negative. I'm afraid nothing about being motivated to create *out of love* even hints that there would be this distinction between a life-friendly place and a life-hostile place as a product of such a creation act. Why even have such a distinction? Moreover, there is a huge moral difference between setting a technological or intellectual challenge before one's child and actively and intentionally crafting a place that is positively deadly to that child.

So, you need an argument for the conclusion that the hostile-to-friendly distinction (and mind-boggling proportion) is as probable or more probable on theism than on atheism, which, as I've argued, is rather high.

Randal: Justin, you said that "atheism would suggest that a majority of the universe would likely not be life-friendly." That statement looks ad hoc to me. Why do you stop at the majority? Why not go the whole way and say that on atheism you would expect that the *totality* of the universe would be hostile to life? And, if you would say that, then it would seem that the fact that the universe *isn't* totally hostile to life, that it includes such hospitable environs as planet earth, is a major *problem* for your view, no?

Justin: That's an important question. Presenting arguments informally in this way can cause me to fail to be explicit on some important details.

Randal: I agree. It's one thing to read off a written argument to a passive audience. It's another thing to have a rough-and-tumble, on-the-fly dialogue and debate over cocktails and goblets of barley wine.

Justin: Right. So, recall that we began this part of our conversation with a skyscraper analogy in which Adam's existence was a part of the background information. The question at the end of that story was regarding how the observation in question (the poison gas) should affect Adam's views of his father's moral character.

Now, with regard to the facts about the hostility of the universe toward life, the question is whether these facts should constitute, for us humans, some evidence for or against God's existence. In the argument then, our very existence is taken as background information—we are the *Adam* of the argument. But, if human existence is being taken as background information, then it follows that the universe is, at least in part, capable of supporting life and is therefore not thoroughly hostile to it. I should have made that more explicit.

Randal: Darn right you should've!

Justin: So, no, I do not consider this to be a major problem for my view. I don't consider it to be a problem at all.

DOES ATHEISM PREDICT A UNIVERSE LESS HOSPITABLE TO LIFE?

Randal: Very good. That's helpful. (But then, you're always helpful *eventually*, so perhaps I shouldn't be surprised!) I certainly agree that human existence is background information in your argument, from which it follows that the universe isn't completely hostile to life. After all, if it *were* completely hostile to life, we wouldn't be having this conversation!

But I don't see that this negates my response. You see, you want to present the fact that the universe is *largely hostile* to life as a problem for theism. I, on the other hand, am suggesting the fact that the universe is *not completely hostile* to life is a problem for atheism.

Justin: Okay, fair enough. Could you further unpack that line of thought so I know exactly what you're claiming and why?

Randal: No problemo compadre.

You believe that if theism is true then we should expect the universe to be *more* hospitable to life than it is. I'm countering that if atheism is true then we should expect the universe to be *less* hospitable to life than it is.

You might call it a tit-for-tat response, in which my clever rejoinder negates the strength of your original point since the precise balance of hostile to hospitable conditions is neither what a theist nor an atheist would expect at first blush.

Justin: Okay. So, I've argued that, given the fact that life exists, the hostility to life of the vast majority of the universe is more easily explained on atheism than on theism.

Your claim is that the fact that life exists at all is more easily explained on theism than on atheism because you think, on atheism, the universe would be entirely hostile to life.

In essence, you're apparently not denying that my argument contains evidence against theism. You're just saying it's not the whole story, and of course I agree. There are a ton of arguments on all sides to consider on questions of the existence of God.

However, if your point here is to, as you claim, "negate the strength of [my] original point," the onus is on you to show that your "hostility argument" for theism is stronger or equal in strength to my "hostility argument" for atheism.

Randal: But why is the onus just on me? Shouldn't it be on both of us? We're *both* looking at the same data, the relative balance of hostile to hospitable elements in the universe, and we're drawing very different conclusions from it. You argue that it favors atheism. But I don't agree.

Justin: Perhaps we're talking past each other. If *all* you're claiming with your use of *negate* here is that, when we ignore the fact that life does exist, the very existence of some life-friendly parts of the universe constitutes *some* evidence favoring a theistic conclusion, that's fine. I've never argued it was impossible for other facts to point in the other direction.

Randal: As I said, theists need not think God created the universe primarily *for* human beings, or any other sentient life for that matter. So we shouldn't *expect* the universe to be on the whole hospitable to human beings.

At the same time, one *would* reasonably expect that God would create environments in which human beings or other sentient life can flourish. And lo and behold, that's what we do, in fact, find!

Justin: We can find agreement in that, if God exists and she has created a universe, there would be environments in which human beings—if they too were created—would be capable of flourishing.

However, your *other* claim—that we shouldn't be surprised if the vast majority of the universe is completely hostile *despite* its having been created out of love—suggests to me that you use that word in a way quite foreign to most people. What about *your* concept of love suggests that an earth-like environment is likely to be placed in an infinitely large and utterly hostile context rather than, say, it just existing by itself or in a far more neutral larger context?

BUT WHY DID GOD CREATE AT ALL?

Randal: I've provided two replies to that question.

First, to reiterate, I've insisted that it is no part of theism to believe God created the universe *just for us* or even *primarily for us*. So it is simply mistaken to have *any* expectation that the universe on the whole would be hospitable to human life. Imagine, by analogy, that a mother stocks her children's playroom with toy cars and dolls. Her son might be indignant because he doesn't care for dolls. He might think, "If mom was really loving to me, surely she would include only toy cars." The problem with the boy's thought process is that the room isn't just for him. It's for his sister as well. And *she likes dolls*. By analogy, the universe isn't just for humans or even primarily for humans. Thus, we should have no expectation that it should be on balance hospitable to human life.

Justin: Randal, then what was the universe created *for*? Can you give an answer to that? If not, how is theism supposed to do any explaining here?

Randal: I don't know all of what it was created for. I wouldn't be surprised if the universe was created for *many* reasons. But my rebuttal to you doesn't depend on me knowing those reasons.

Justin: That's just plain false. My argument was that this hostility is *better explained* on an atheistic hypothesis than a theistic one. The fact that you cannot provide God's sole or even primary reason(s) for creating the universe should not strike readers as anything resembling a rebuttal. If God's reasons for creating are mysterious, they are, at the very least, a poorer explanation for the hostility we see than is atheism.

Randal: "Plain false?!" Are you kiddin' me? And hey, you don't tell our readers what they're supposed to think! Let them draw their own conclusions!

Justin: Okay, I'll stop with all this airtight logical nudging.

Randal: Ah, so that's what it was. Sorry, I missed that!

Anyway, I *did* suggest *one* of the reasons for God's creating this severe and beautiful universe that is broadly inhospitable to human life: it provides a unique opportunity for the inestimable goods of human exploration and discovery. But that's merely *one* of innumerable reasons God could have to create in the manner he did.

Justin: But if the earth *already* contains a nearly insurmountable number of intellectual and exploratory challenges, then compounding that infinitely is at best superfluous and at worst a distraction.

Moreover, as I've already mentioned, there is a huge moral difference between setting a technological, exploratory, or other intellectual challenge before one's child and actively, purposefully crafting a place that is positively *deadly* to that child in an effort to encourage exploration.

In other words, one can encourage exploration without the use of a giant death trap. This is doubly true for cosmic parents with the gift of infinite power.

Randal: Whoa, wait a minute! You think placing challenges beyond planet earth is superfluous at best and a distraction at worst? So should we think that Columbus's discovery of America was a great achievement but Neil Armstrong's walking on the moon was merely a *distraction*?

I see things quite the opposite. Each step of exploration that we take is even *greater* than the one that came before. For goodness sake, we could join Mark Watney in visiting Mars in the next decade and achieving inestimable goods as individuals and a species as we do so. How amazing that would be! And that's just the beginning. To quote *Toy Story*'s Buzz Lightyear, "To infinity . . . and beyond!" Who can imagine the goods our species can achieve by taking on these exploratory challenges in the coming decades and centuries? And all because the universe offers a challenge that is vast and hostile, like the harsh and beautiful upper slopes of Mount Everest, but multiplied by unimaginable orders of magnitude.

Justin: Heed my words more closely. I said compounding these investigations to *infinity* is what's superfluous. I'm all for scientific exploration, and I'd agree with you that a virtuous God would be as well. But that does no work toward explaining why 99 percent of the universe is so hostile to life. I'd like to think a good God has ways to challenge us toward exploration without subjecting us to an infinite death trap of darkness.

Randal: "Infinite death trap of darkness"?! Hah! That's so dramatic, it sounds like a Scandinavian death metal band: "Did you hear the latest album from *Infinite Death Trap of Darkness*? Amazing guitar work!"

Justin: A classic.

Randal: Look, I agree that God could have other ways to challenge us. But that's irrelevant. The point is that it is fully consistent with God's existence that he chose *this way* to challenge us.

Justin: The fact that God could have presented us the same kinds of challenges while making the universe *less* hostile to moral agents is irrelevant? I beg to differ. If a morally upright person is to choose between two different ways of knowingly achieving the same goal, they will, in accordance with their moral nature, choose the less harmful route.

Moreover, I've never claimed that choosing "this way" to challenge us was *inconsistent* with God's existence. My claim was far humbler. I merely claimed that, given that life exists in the universe, the hostility of the vast majority of it is more to be expected on atheism than it is on theism.

In this chapter, I've consistently maintained that, given that moral agents exist, atheism better explains the near universal hostility of our universe than does theism. Given that theism does not lead us to expect, prior to observing our surroundings, a distinction between the friendly parts of God's creation and hostile parts of God's creation, appeals to a purposeful *safe house* within a wider, dangerous region are, as I've argued, woefully ad hoc. Moreover, if, on theism, the reason(s) for which the universe was created are not available to us, we are not entitled to posit it as a serious explanation of the observations under consideration.

Randal: As I said, your intuition that we should expect God to make a universe that is broadly hospitable for human beings can't even get off the ground unless you assume that God created the universe primarily for human beings, *which I don't.*

Consider this *cool* analogy. Imagine two polar bears, Koda and Snowflake, having a debate about whether there is a zoo designer who purposefully designed the zoo they live in. Koda insists there isn't a zoo designer. The reason? He points out that most of the zoo is not hospitable to polar bears. (What's with that steaming jungle habitat? And the aviary? What a waste of space!) And surely, Koda reasons, if there *were* a zoo designer, he/she *would* make it mostly hospitable to polar bears.

You'd think, right? But Snowflake demurs, as she points out that Koda's objection only works *if one assumes that the zoo was designed primarily to serve the needs of polar bears.* And Snowflake *doesn't* accept that assumption. In her view, maintaining a safe and hospitable environment for polar bears is only one of many purposes for the zoo. And thus, by Snowflake's estimation, Koda's assumptions (and the argument that goes with them) are flawed from the outset.

I gotta tell you, I'm with Snowflake on this one! Your argument parallels Koda's, and it's flawed for the same reason.

Justin: Since, to our knowledge thus far, the universe is not like a zoo with many different habitats for many different creatures, such a story won't get us far. You've continuously claimed that my argument requires the premise that the universe was primarily created for humans. But again, *nobody* needs to assume that humans, or even life in general, were the primary reason(s) for creating the universe in order for this argument to go through. All they need to assume is that God loves humans as her children, and that whatever non-human motivating reason for the universe there is could be fulfilled by an omnipotent being *without* making 99 percent of the universe completely hostile to those whom she loves as children and most other forms of life that we know of.

Curiously, there are *some* forms of life that are able to get along fine in most of the universe. If God exists, she has created *some* creatures with that ability while also deciding *against* giving *moral agents* that ability, even though, presumably, they are the pinnacle of terrestrial life on theism. Strange priorities.

It seems as though, once again, we've come up to a dead end. Our intuitions diverge radically on this question of what we as humans should expect to find in our universe. I've argued that we should not see so much hostility toward life. You've argued that I've no basis for such a judgment.

Randal: I need to start by replying to your critique of the zoo analogy. It doesn't require that each "habitat" in the universe include sentient creatures. It only requires that the sentient life in question (human beings or polar bears) is restricted to one part of the realm (universe or zoo).

Be that as it may, you're right that once again we come up to a dead end of sorts. But I will say I am grateful for you presenting this argument because I believe the intuitions to which you appeal are widespread in the skeptic/atheist community. I have often encountered skeptics of theism invoking the size, age, and hostility of the universe to life as evidence against a creator God. I suspect Carl Sagan's eloquent and existentially jolting ruminations about our "pale blue dot" have contributed as much to skepticism in the last thirty years as anything.[6] And it seems to me that your argument provides a good start at clarifying and defending the intuitions at work, even if I remain unconvinced.

Justin: With this topic having come to completion, it would appear we are again free to explore yet another issue.

Randal: By Jove, I think you're right!

Justin: Is there some other observation you think counts as evidence for theism that you think might be worth exploring?

Chapter 6

GOD, MATHEMATICS, AND REASON

Randal: Indeed, there is! You started the discussion about the hostility of the universe with the illustration of a young man living in a house. I, too, would like to begin with an illustration that draws an analogy between the universe and a house. But in my telling the focus and lesson will be rather different.

Justin: Is it safe to assume this one isn't spouting poisonous gas?

Randal: Heh heh, you'd be right in that assumption. I'm going to keep this analogy simple, with no bells or whistles (or poison gas).

Perhaps I can start by giving you the basic idea, and then we can unpack it from a couple of different angles.

Justin: Certainly. I'm ready to hear what you have to offer.

ON THE UNREASONABLE EFFECTIVENESS OF MATHEMATICS

Randal: Excellent. So I think I'll begin with a famous essay by theoretical physicist Eugene Wigner. In that essay, titled "The Unreasonable Effectiveness of Mathematics in the Natural Sciences," Wigner reflects on the astounding degree to which the universe can be described in mathematical terms. He writes, "The miracle of the appropriateness of the language of mathematics for the formulation of the laws of physics is a wonderful gift which we neither understand nor deserve."[1]

I agree with Wigner that this is a wonderful gift, but from a theistic perspective it is neither unexpected nor unreasonable. Since the theist believes the universe to be the product of a benevolent, rational mind, it is no surprise that, just as the architect and engineer would design a house according to a precise mathematical blueprint, so a rational God should design a universe according to

153

a precise mathematical blueprint, one that is decipherable by finite, rational minds.

But it seems to me that that which fits so well within a theistic worldview is fundamentally inexplicable within an atheistic one.

Justin: Hmm. You and Wigner have found it fitting to describe this appropriateness of mathematical language as a *gift*. Surely this choice in rhetoric needs to be recognized as just that.

Randal: Whoa, presumably you're using the term *rhetoric* as a pejorative here. That seems unduly harsh. To be sure, Wigner is speaking figuratively, but he certainly isn't engaged in the bombast of mere rhetoric.

Justin: My point was to identify the loaded wording in a stated premise. What I'm more concerned with is why this appropriateness of mathematics is to be, as you say, "fundamentally inexplicable" within an atheistic view? Atheism is, after all, compatible with a number of views about mathematics, including Platonist views of mathematics, where mathematic entities are abstract and exist independently of our thinking about them. Needless to say, this strikes me as a bold claim, and I'll need some help tracking with you here.

Randal: Have patience, my friend. All shall be revealed!

How about I start by making some observations about the astounding mathematical structure of the world? And then you and I can each offer our reflections on how we explain that structure in light of our worldview.

Justin: Sure thing. Let's hear it.

NUMERICAL PATTERNS AS ARCHITECTURAL MOTIFS

Randal: Okay, on to numbers in nature. Let's start with the famed Fibonacci number sequence. This is a numerical pattern that begins with 0, 1, 1, and then from there every subsequent integer in the sequence is the combination of the previous two: 0, 1, 1, 2, 3, 5, 8, 13, 21, and on to infinity.

You often find the Fibonacci sequence in human designs. But the astounding fact is that you also find this pattern throughout nature, ranging from the spiral structure of seashells and pinecones to pinwheel galaxies. The petal numbers of flowers regularly conform to one of the Fibonacci numbers. You can also find the Fibonacci sequence in tree branches, cabbages, sunflower seeds, pineapples, artichokes, bees, music, reflections, and countless other areas.[2] Like a meadow awash in wildflowers, the natural world is blooming with the patterns of the Fibonacci sequence.

Justin: Thanks for that. I suppose it might be good if you were to get more specific on one example of the sequence found in nature. Then we can discuss why you think of it as evidence for theism.

Randal: If you don't mind, instead I'd like to introduce another recurring mathematical pattern: pi (3.14). As we all know, pi is the ratio of the circumference of a circle to its diameter. And so, pi is stamped on nature every time you find a circular structure, from the DNA double helix spiral to the splash in a pond.

But that's only the beginning. Like the Fibonacci sequence, pi appears in places that you'd never expect. For example, in 1996, Hans-Henrik Stolum published a paper in *Science* in which he argued that the average meandering ratio[3] for rivers is pi.[4]

Pi also makes appearances in probability theory. For example, if you drop a needle on a grid with parallel lines, where the width between the lines is equivalent to the length of the needle, the likelihood that the needle will fall on a line rather than in the spaces between is 2/pi.

These are just a few examples of the innumerable, fascinating instances of pi in nature. Time and again, this numerical value pops up in the strangest places. On the *Nova* documentary *The Great Math Mystery*, the narrator observes, "One writer has suggested it's like seeing pi on a series of mountain peaks, poking out of a fog shrouded valley. We know there is a way they're all connected but it's not always obvious how."[5]

There are still other recurring mathematical patterns in nature as well, such as the golden ratio, but I don't want to belabor the point. Suffice it to say, the ubiquity of numerical patterns like the Fibonacci sequence and pi (and the golden ratio) throughout nature has led mathematicians to exclaim in wonder that math is the language of the universe. And the question for us is this: which worldview fits best with the incredible mathematical structure of the world? In particular, is the recurrence of these mathematical patterns throughout nature more to be expected on atheism or on theism?

Justin: You've laid out some examples of things in nature that resemble some mathematical sequences or patterns. Very well. You seem to want to suggest that these patterns (or their applicability?) are more surprising on atheism than they are on theism, but I need to hear more of your thought process on this because, at present, it's all still a bit too vague for my liking.

Randal: But of course!

Justin: I'm glad to hear there's more.

Randal: There's *always* more, amigo.

So here's the idea: We begin with the fact that, on theism, the universe is brought into being by God. That means that God functions analogically to an architect. Just as an architect plans a building and then oversees its construction, so God plans creation and then oversees its construction. Theologians even have a term for the planning stage of creation. They call it the divine decree. So God decrees (plans), and then God creates (builds).[6]

Justin: Well, I think we need to exercise a bit of caution with this comparison, especially with whatever implications we draw from it. But I'll shut up. Go on.

Randal: Your reservations have been noted!

With that in mind, we would expect creation to exhibit some features that are analogical to the buildings that are designed and constructed by architects. One of the most common elements of architectural design is the design motif, a recurring structured pattern. There are countless architectural design motifs: geometric patterns, meanders, rosettes, ornaments, and so on. Often the motifs in question serve as a creative signature of the artist. My favorite example is the famed Spanish architect Antoni Gaudi, whose work is imbued by motifs drawn from nature in an inimitable signature style, nowhere more so than in his greatest work, the magnificent Sagrada Familia Church in Barcelona.

If God functions like an architect, then just as the architect incorporates design motifs into his/her work, so we would expect God to incorporate design motifs into his work. So when we find recurring mathematical patterns throughout nature, patterns like the Fibonacci sequence, pi, and the golden ratio, we find exactly the kind of patterns that would serve as divine design motifs. In short, these are the kind of complex mathematical patterns one might expect to find in nature if the universe were indeed created by God. But if there is no God then such patterns become perplexing, inexplicable, brute facts.

Justin: Okay, that helps me with understanding where you were going with this argument. For starters, I will agree with you that, *if* God exists and has created the world, then, in that sense, she functions in similar ways to an architect. But I don't think there is any basis for assuming God would be likely to behave like human architects. There are a number of differences.

Randal: Do tell!

Justin: For one, unlike human architects, God does not simply reshape preexisting building materials. Rather, God is supposed to have created from absolutely nothing. Secondly, artists leave these little motifs as a kind of signature to distinguish their works from other works or to distinguish that style from other styles. Expecting this behavior from a creative agent makes sense only if there are preexisting styles of concrete objects from which God might wish to distinguish her handiwork. But this is not the case at the point of God's creative decree.

Unlike the creations of human architects, every object or design that God creates is utterly original. There are no antecedents. For any object God creates at that very first moment, nothing of a similar theme, makeup, or purpose has ever existed prior to its coming into existence. To be sure, I am not claiming that God wouldn't put these personal signatures on her works if she existed. I am only claiming that we have no clue if she would and that the human analogy is uninformative for at least these reasons.

Randal: I'm glad you agree that God's relationship to creation is analogous to an architect's relationship to the building she creates. But what about your points of disanalogy? Of the points you raise, it seems to me the most important one is your claim that motifs are only included as a means to distinguish an architect's work from other works and other styles. As you said, "Expecting this behavior from a creative agent makes sense only if there are preexisting styles of concrete objects from which God might wish to distinguish his handiwork."

While I agree with you that an identifying "artistic signature" provides *one* reason why one might include architectural motifs in their work, it certainly isn't the only reason.

Imagine, for a moment, that there is a great architect living on an isolated tropical island that has no contact with the outside world. She designs all the buildings on the island so that the population of the community is exposed to no designs other than those of their resident architect. Given that there are no other competing architects, does it follow that she will include no design motifs in her work? Not at all. She could still have many reasons for including motifs in her work. For example, she might include rosettes for no other reason than that *she likes rosettes.*

Just as an architect can have endless reasons for including design motifs in her work apart from the need to distinguish her work from that of competing architects, so God could have endless reasons for including design motifs in his work apart from the need to distinguish that work from competing creators. The point is that *theism explains the presence of these perplexing recurring mathematical patterns as architectural design motifs.*

By contrast, I don't see that atheism offers *any* explanation for patterns like the Fibonacci sequence or pi. Do you?

DEBATING THE ARCHITECTURAL MOTIF ARGUMENT

Justin: That's a fine response, but, of course, I never claimed that God couldn't have other reasons to place motifs in her work. I was only pointing out that the reason *you* gave doesn't actually apply so it doesn't serve as a *positive* reason for why God is likely to create motifs. There may of course be other reasons for creating design motifs, but I assume you want to demonstrate something more than God being consistent with the observations.

On the other hand, given regular, simple laws, we'd expect repeating patterns to appear quite often in nature on atheism so it's still not clear to me why this should be seen as evidence for theism. Do you have a reason to suggest divine psychology has some interest in Fibonacci sequences or pi specifically rather than some very different but equally arbitrary pattern or patterns? I ask because, if God has no Fibonacci or pi-based fetish, then do you consider all patterns and numbers in nature as evidence for God?

Randal: Hmm, you say that I haven't established that God would have something like a "Fibonacci or pi-based fetish" that might explain the repetition of the Fibonacci sequence and pi in particular. But this is a misrepresentation of my argument.

Justin: I'm not sure I follow. Please explain.

Randal: I never set out to explain why pi and the Fibonacci sequence *in particular* are repeated in nature. Rather, I set out to explain *why in general complex mathematical patterns like pi and the Fibonacci sequence* are repeated in nature. And I've presented an explanation by attributing them to a divine architect who includes architectural motifs in his work in analogy to the motifs of a human architect.

Justin: Ah, well, I misunderstood the scope of the argument then.

Randal: All is forgiven.

Justin: I must say, though, the same point applies. You need a reason for why God would be likely to repeat complex yet ultimately arbitrary mathematical patterns in her creation. Your repeated invoking of the tendencies of creativity among humans is problematic for the reasons I've already discussed.

Randal: I never said these mathematical patterns are *arbitrary*. Just as a human architect has her reasons, so does God.

Justin: As you've been quick to admit throughout our extended conversation, God is not like humans. We shouldn't be so quick to import contingencies of human creativity to the divine. In other words, yes, your architect, if she likes rosettes, may repeatedly create rosettes. But we can't just pretend that positing the creative activity of a particular architect as the explanation of those rosettes has any explanatory power unless we *also* happen know that she really is particularly fond of that design.

In the same way, without independent reasons for thinking that God is fond of the kinds of general complexities you're actually referring to, then positing her creative activity lacks the guts we typically look for in a good explanation.

Randal: Justin, it pains me to say this, but that's simply not true.

Justin: Ah, but it pains me even *more*.

Randal: You don't need to know *why* an architect utilizes a particular design motif to know *that* he or she utilizes it. I can be familiar with the major motifs in Gaudi's architecture, for example, without knowing *why* he included these motifs. Similarly, one can reasonably conclude *that* God utilized particular design motifs in creation without knowing why he did so.

Justin: It is certainly true that we don't need to know *exactly* why some designer created a feature to know *that* a designer did, in fact, create it. That said, if one wants to posit God as an *explanation* of some group of patterns or motifs, then you need a reason why God would create those rather than something entirely different.

Randal: My point is that those types of patterns are not surprising on theism, but they are on atheism. Now I want to come back to your atheist rejoinder in which you seek to offer your own explanation of these recurring patterns. You say that all you need are some simple laws that can explain the repeating patterns of the Fibonacci sequence and pi (and the golden ratio and who knows what else). That's very helpful, *just so long as you can explain what those simple laws are and why they should obtain rather than some other laws.* If you can't do that, then your rejoinder is nothing more than a promissory note to have faith that an explanation consistent with atheism shall be forthcoming in the future. And I hope you'll forgive me if I don't, as yet, have *that much* faith.

Justin: Your argument, as you've stated above, is *not* about pi or the Fibonacci sequence in *particular* being repeated in nature. Rather, you're interested in *why in general complex mathematical patterns like them* are repeated in nature.

But what about your lack of trust in science either already having or coming up with some future explanation for these repeated mathematical patterns?

Here I'll quote the Sith Lord and Supreme Commander of the Imperial fleet himself: "I find your lack of faith disturbing."

Randal: Chastised for lack of faith? Well now, *that's* something you don't hear from an atheist every day!

Justin: Yes, it might sound strange coming from an atheist, but, remember, at the beginning of this dialogue we chose to define faith as roughly equivalent to *trust*. And, well, if there are strong reasons for trusting that some proposition is true, then it may be rational to accept it as true.

Randal: Hold on, it isn't that you and I agreed together to define faith as roughly equivalent to trust. Rather, I pointed out there are two common definitions of faith, with trust being one of them. Anyway, I'm just heartened to hear an atheist chastising me for lack of faith!

In the absence of a clever Jedi rejoinder to the Sith Lord, let me offer a couple more sober responses.

Let me start by illustrating how weak your appeal to faith is by presenting an analogy. Imagine if the prosecutor in a murder trial provided evidence that the DNA of the accused was found on the murder weapon. That's exactly the kind of evidence one would expect if the defendant were guilty, and so it would seem to support the prosecution's case. Now imagine if all that the defense said in rebuttal was that they had faith that in the future forensics will one day show that kind of DNA evidence to be unreliable. That wouldn't get very far with the jury! Courts depend on evidence and argument. They don't ask juries to defer to faith in the absence of evidence. And, yet, that's what you're asking here. You ask us to defer to the hope that my argument will eventually be defeated by the advance of science.

Justin: Yes, of course. If he stopped there, I agree his comments *would* rightly be met with confusion or scorn.

For that reason, I need to have room to provide my *reason* for saying we can rationally have trust in science's ability to explain some observation. Given the one-way trend of scientific explanations replacing supernaturalistic explanations, we have good probabilistic reasons for thinking that it will be a mere matter of time. So, if it really is the case that we don't know the answer to some scientific question, historical precedent makes it rational for us to think one will eventually be found without any appeal to supernatural forces. At the very least, the dismal record of explanation-based theistic research programs should lead us to be dubious about theism's future explanatory success.

You seem to suggest, though, that we would need such a hope to defeat your argument. I must disagree here. I think it's clear by now that you've failed to argue that theism would lead us to expect complex mathematical patterns more than atheism, and so your argument really does boil down to a God-of-the-gaps argument. That is to say, you've claimed to have found a place of scientific ignorance, and you've plugged in a hypothesis with no explanatory power with respect to complex mathematics. With all due respect, this just isn't a very good argument.

Randal: I haven't invoked, as you say, a "theistic research program" any more than you've invoked an "atheistic research program." I've simply argued that theism better explains one aspect of the natural world just as you've denied this. The problem is that it seems that you now want to exclude appeal to divine explanations *a priori* because of their alleged poor track record. In that case, I must wonder why you even entered into this conversation in the first place. Whatever issue I might raise, you can just defer to your unshakeable faith that science will explain it eventually. Atheists sometimes chide Christians for having superficial "God-did-it" explanations. Well it seems like you're going for a "science-will-do-it" equivalent.

Justin: I agree that you have not invoked an entire theistic research program. I've never claimed otherwise. Your attempt at explaining observations in the world by positing a particular kind of explanation (the creative powers of God) is just the latest in a long, unsuccessful history. When comparing different explanations, this stain of a historical precedent about theistic explanations in general should count for something.

Randal: The stain of history? Yikes, I hope that washes out.

Justin: I'm not sure why you think I've attempted to exclude divine explanations a priori. I believe we've walked through a number of arguments while comparing the explanatory merits of theism. The historical precedent to which I am referring is nothing like an a priori dismissal; rather, it's recognizing that a track record should count.

Randal: You talk about a *track record*, but *which* track record? I'm not proposing theistic explanations of *nature*, for therein lies the realm of natural science. Rather, I'm offering an explanation in philosophy, and specifically metaphysics, and appeals to God have a rich and honorable place in metaphysical explanation.

Anyway, you're quite mistaken to think that identifying one of your hoped-for pattern-generating natural laws would address my challenge. It wouldn't. Let's assume for a moment that science does uncover laws that explain how it is that, for example, flower petal numbers tend to conform to the Fibonacci sequence. As I said, even in this case *you'd still need to explain why these physical laws obtain rather than some other physical laws.* In other words, you'd merely have pushed the question back a step. In that case, the question would shift to this: why is the world structured with physical laws that manifest complex mathematical patterns throughout nature?

In short, the problem remains.

Justin: Yeah, I don't agree with that at all. One does not need to explain the purported explanation in order to show that it is the better of the two on offer.

But let's look closer at the piece of evidence you've brought up repeatedly, so that we can address it once and for all. You point to the number of flower petals as being Fibonacci numbers and say this is somehow an interesting fact about nature that demands an explanation. Cell biologist Todd Cooke of the University of Maryland observes,

> The numbers 2, 3, and 5 (and their multiples) are frequently alleged to disclose the involvement of the Fibonacci sequence in a given process because they are taken to represent unique Fibonacci numbers as opposed to other "non-Fibonacci" numbers. It follows from this allegation that any structure appearing in a group of five, such as the digits on the human hand or the petals on a rose flower, can be interpreted as being a manifestation of the Fibonacci sequence. But the first six positive integers are either components or multiples of the primary Fibonacci sequence; thus, a small group must be composed of at least 7 units before it appears to be unrelated to the primary Fibonacci sequence.[7]

Science writer Philip Ball writes, "Even if we consider numbers up to 21, only four (7, 11, 17, 19) are not Fibonacci numbers or multiples of them. No wonder we see Fibonacci numbers everywhere!"[8]

Randal: In the first passage you quote, Todd Cooke is not rebutting the presence or significance of Fibonacci sequences in nature. He's merely challenging the attempt to find Fibonacci sequences in phyllotactic patterns (that is, the arrangement of petals, leaves, and branches). That does nothing to explain the extraordinary presence of Fibonacci sequence patterns in everything from seashells to spiral galaxies. And of course it also says nothing about other recurring mathematical patterns, like pi and the golden ratio. It is also incorrect to suggest that I placed particular stock in that one particular example.

But I assume you're after something more ambitious than a quibble over one example. Are you attempting to *generalize* Cooke's point by claiming that *all* instances of recurring mathematical patterns in nature are nothing more than the projection of these patterns onto nature—patterns that really only exist in our minds?

Justin: You're right that he isn't challenging the idea that Fibonacci numbers show up in nature. Rather, he is challenging the notion that this particular example suggests anything beyond ordinary natural forces. As Ball notes, to some degree, it's actually quite difficult to avoid Fibonacci numbers.

Needless to say, I'm not interested in generalizing the problem with *this* example over all of the examples you've claimed, nor am I qualified, as a nonexpert, to play whack-a-mole with every post hoc numerological assertion one could make about "designs" in our world. However, given that it was the example you cited a number of times now, I figured it was one you found particularly interesting.

Randal: Hmm, that's an interesting take on the matter, given that I placed no special emphasis on that particular example. And I'm not so sure about your general characterization either. Whack-a-mole is a game children play at Chuck E. Cheese's. But I take it we're engaged in a serious discussion of a range of phenomena that are supposedly surprising on atheism but not on theism.

Justin: While whack-a-mole may be fun at your best friend's eighth birthday party, it's considerably less so in the context of an argument.

Randal: Sorry, I don't have any eight-year-old friends. And note that I didn't accuse *you* of playing whack-a-mole when you introduced a range of examples of cosmic hostility that you wanted me to explain.

So I'm not sure why you think I'm playing whack-a-mole when I offer a range of evidential examples to support *my* thesis!

Justin: What your argument consists of is a broad claim about complex mathematics in nature, for which you have several examples. Given that I am not an expert in biochemistry or any of the other possibly relevant fields, I can't really speak as to whether these claims represent *genuine mysteries* among relevant scientific experts. To be quite frank, I doubt they do.

That said, if the history of theistic explanations is to shed any light on this conversation, it is that this general gap-filling strategy is probably a dead end.

Randal: Decrying this argument as mere "gap-filling" appears to me to be nothing more than an attempt to tar me with a rhetorical brush. You're still not grappling with the force of the argument. As I said, the argument includes the need to explain laws of nature that are fine-tuned to reflect these complex recurring numerical patterns. Being an expert in biochemistry or any other field of natural science is not going to help you with a metaphysical explanation, given that scientists *begin* with the laws of nature such as they are. Thus, the discovery of a natural law to account for the genesis of these patterns would merely invite the follow-up question of whether natural laws that generate recurring high-level mathematical patterns in nature are more to be expected on theism or atheism.

WHY EXPLANATIONS NEED NOT HAVE THEIR OWN EXPLANATION

Randal: So, once again, it looks like we're stalled.

But even so, I'm not ready to leave the topic behind just yet. At the outset of this conversation I said that I wanted to approach the issue from a couple of angles. The analogy of an architectural motif is only the first. So are you okay if we leave this specific argument behind and move onto my related argument?

Justin: I'm fine with that. Though I do think it's important to repeat that one does not need to give a more fundamental explanation of a proposed explanation in order to show that it is a *better* explanation.

Randal: Right, you did say that.

Justin: Philosopher Gregory Dawes writes,

> Richard Dawkins, for instance, writes that to explain the machinery of life "by invoking a supernatural Designer is to explain precisely nothing." Why? Because it "leaves unexplained the origin of the designer." . . . Dawkins apparently assumes that every successful explanation should also explain its own *explanans*. But this is an unreasonable demand. Many of our most successful explanations raise new puzzles and present us with new questions to be answered.[9]

In the same way, one could posit an earthquake to explain why the pictures have fallen off the shelf. It serves as a plausible explanation regardless of the fact that it hasn't addressed the antecedent issue of why that earthquake happened in that place and at that time.

Randal: I agree with all that. And I'm especially heartened by your taking a dig at Richard Dawkins's shoddy reasoning in *The God Delusion*. His central argument against God is not a good one, and that's one reason why.

The example is spot on. An earthquake would provide a good explanation for pictures falling off a shelf, and you don't need to explain what caused the earthquake before you can say that the earthquake caused the pictures to fall. Indeed, to require such a thing would quickly lead to an infinite regress of explanations, which is absurd. So on that much we agree.

That said, I need to ask, how is atheism relevantly analogous to the earthquake? I see perfectly well how an earthquake would explain the fallen pictures. But how does atheism explain the complex, recurring numerical patterns we find throughout nature? If I understand you correctly, to this point you've stated that at least some of these patterns (e.g., some instances of the Fibonacci sequence) are not in need of explanation and the rest will one day be explained by science. But I don't see appeals to hoped-for future explanations as having *any* present explanatory value analogous to the earthquake hypothesis.

Justin: That's only been one part of my answer.

Randal: Oh good, I was getting worried.

Justin: My position here is that the natural world as we know it probably explains these issues by way of known scientific processes. Again, I'm not in a position to say with supreme confidence whether the myriad examples you've provided are genuine mysteries to the relevant scientific communities.

But again, I doubt it.

I've also consistently said that, *even if they are mysteries,* consistent historical trends suggest that they are likely to have an explanation in the future and that God-of-the-gaps arguments like this one fall in time. This pessimistic attitude toward your argument is not unfounded. While these patterns in nature may be interesting, I've not been given a substantive, non-ad-hoc reason why this is more to be expected on theism than on an atheistic hypothesis.

So yes, another stand-off it is.

THE MATHEMATICAL BLUEPRINT ARGUMENT

Randal: Fair enough, though it is simply confused to label a metaphysical argument like this as God-of-the-gaps. Beyond that, I could repeat why I still think you're wrong, and you could reply by reiterating why you think I'm wrong, but that would probably get boring after a while. So let's just move on to my second argument. This is a broader argument, which shifts away from isolated mathematical patterns to the extraordinary degree to which mathematics generally maps onto physical reality. And, once again, I'd like to build my case on a thought experiment.

Justin: Alright, let's hear it.

Randal: So imagine walking in the rough high country when you come upon a curious arrangement of rocks. Their unusual placement is suggestive of design, but the appearance is not itself sufficient to warrant that conclusion, and so you withhold judgment. However, as you study the formation more closely you discover the extraordinary fact that at noon on the winter solstice the sun shines directly through a hole in the peak of the highest obelisk and lands directly in the middle of a circle of rocks right in the center of the formation. It is fair to say that this discovery would constitute a remarkable fit between the rock structure and astronomical phenomena, a fit that would cry out for an intelligent explanation.

Justin: I should briefly interject here as I'm highly skeptical of this design inference.

Randal: Why am I not surprised?

Justin: A small grouping of rocks casting a shadow on another at a time on which humans have *imposed* meaning is, well, going to be as frequent as our imagination's ability to attach meaning to ultimately meaningless astronomical happenings. Perhaps I've got a fence post out front whose shadow points toward the exact center of my neighbor's garage door at ten a.m. on the anniversary of his college roommate's fifth marriage. I'm not sure this "calls out" for an explanation.

But I'll shut up and let you make your broader point.

Randal: No need to shut up in this case. After all, I share your skepticism on the fencepost. As for the scenario *I* painted, if the sun shone through the hole in that obelisk at 3:41 p.m. on a Tuesday, folks would rightly dismiss it as insignificant. But the winter solstice is not merely significant because we arbitrarily imbue it with meaning. It's the lowest excursion on the celestial sphere relative to the celestial equator. If the sun shone through the hole at noon on the winter solstice, that is *precisely* the kind of fine-grained significant connection to the natural world that would suggest intentional design to the archaeoastronomer.

Justin: Do you see the lowest excursion on the celestial sphere relative to the celestial equator to be something of objective significance? I sure don't, so it doesn't seem designed at all. That said, feel free to continue to make your point.

Randal: Well, I'll let you take up that complaint with the archaeoastronomers, since they certainly *do* find the solstice to be astronomically significant. Indeed, my scenario is based on a real place, which warrants precisely this kind of design inference—the Newgrange prehistoric monument in Ireland. So your quibble really is with experts in the field.

Justin: Sure, it has significance in a particular field. I'm just saying it's no more special *objectively* than any other astronomical happening.

Randal: The point I'm making is not limited to the methods of archaeoastronomy. The general lesson is that we *all* look for finely tuned patterns that are indicative of intelligence. I want to argue that this same principle can be applied to the relationship between the physical world and mathematics. And that was Wigner's point in the famous paper with which I launched this discussion. Just as the rock structure maps onto astronomical reality with an extraordinary fit, so our physical universe maps onto mathematical reality with an extraordinary fit. And just as intelligence is the best explanation of the former, so I believe it is the best explanation of the latter.

Justin: Okay, I think I see where you're going here. It's another design inference. Unfortunately, it's another toward which I am quite dubious. You regard the universe as *mapping onto* mathematical reality. But why endorse that view rather than one that holds that the concepts at play in mathematics map onto our physical reality after the fact—or some other option entirely?

Randal: Let me start by noting that some instances of mathematical mapping are *not* surprising and thus do not require an explanation. For example, Euclid's algorithm enables us to calculate the greatest common divisor between two numbers. It turns out that we can use the algorithm throughout nature, but this *isn't* surprising given that Euclid's algorithm is logically necessary so it *must* apply to any physical universe.

Justin: Okay, sure. Go on.

Randal: But other cases of mathematical mapping are not like that. For example, consider the fact that we can use calculus to map the path of a baseball that is hit by a bat. So long as we have the right initial variables (the height at which the ball was hit, the angle, the initial velocity of the ball, the wind speed, and so on) we can predict the trajectory of the ball with dizzying accuracy.

Justin: Right. Assuming we know both the initial conditions and the number and degree of the forces acting upon it, these things are pretty predictable.

Randal: Yes, but the really important point is that this mapping of the baseball's trajectory is *not* like Euclid's algorithm. You see, there is nothing *logically* necessary about the laws of nature being what they are such that a baseball *must* assume this trajectory when hit.

Justin: Oh, okay. I think I see what you're getting at.

Randal: Nonetheless, we find mathematics provides a powerful tool to plot the ball's course, a fit reminiscent of my analogy of the rock formation to the winter solstice. The natural world is describable in the language of mathematics, and yet it need not have been the case. Once we realize there is no logical or metaphysical necessity here, this particular fit becomes a cause for wonder, as Albert Einstein conceded when he famously observed, "The most incomprehensible thing about the physical world is that it is comprehensible."[10]

Justin: So, this is just an argument about there being regularities in nature?

Randal: No, this is an argument based on the fact that the physical world is richly describable in the language of mathematics. As I said, there is no logical necessity that the natural world be describable mathematically, and yet it is. This calls out for explanation, and a *mind* is precisely the kind of explanation that accounts for the phenomenon.

Justin: Well, hear me out. Imagine a universe quite different from our own, with regular laws quite different from our own. With those regular physical laws acting on your baseball, we would likely still be able to map the trajectory mathematically. With that in view, it matters little that the laws we happen to have are not, as you've mentioned, logically necessary.

This is why I ask whether your argument is really about why we have any regularities. Am I completely off base here?

Randal: Hmm, off base on a baseball illustration. Clever!

So you think Wigner and Einstein were confused to find this mathematical describability to be a surprising fact?

Justin: I'm not saying that at all. I'm saying the particular argument I've been given here isn't something I find terribly compelling.

Randal: Okay, but what is your *basis* for claiming that natural regularities in other possible worlds would likely be describable in the language of mathematics? To be honest, it seems to me that you're trying to avoid the problem I've presented rather than offer a response to it.

Justin: This question just seems bizarre to me. Can you imagine a possible world in which the language of mathematics, a language we invent, is useless to us with regard to describing things? Assuming we exist and are capable of some kind of mathematics, why would we be incapable of creating mathematical concepts and using them to describe the interesting relationships in the world around us?

Randal: Remember, I pointed out that *some degree* of mathematical mapping (e.g., Euclid's algorithm) occurs in every physical world. So that clearly does *not* require an explanation.

The issue is the complex and contingent nature of mathematical mapping that we find in nature. I started with calculus and a mundane baseball example, but that's only the beginning. More than a century ago, Einstein's Special Theory of Relativity predicted the phenomenon of time dilation, that is, that time was not absolute and thus that it could *slow down* under some circumstances. This extraordinary prediction was confirmed in a 2014 experiment in which lithium ions were accelerated in a particle accelerator to one-third the speed of light.[11] Let me say it again: *a 2014 experiment of dizzying sophistication in a particle accelerator confirmed the predictions of complex mathematical equations written out a century before.*

Justin: Yes, that prediction was first confirmed back in 1938 in the Ives-Stilwell experiment. In 2014, however, scientists have confirmed this prediction again but with unprecedented precision!

Given a robust theoretical framework for how some aspect of the physical universe operates, predictions based on that framework will be able to be tested in increasingly precise ways as new methods are devised.

Science is pretty rad.

Randal: Science is indeed amazing, though I must admit that I stopped calling anything *rad* around the same time that grunge music became popular.

Justin: Ouch!

Randal: It could've been worse. At least you didn't say science is *groovy*.

Look, the philosophical question before us is which of these two views, theism or atheism, best explains this highly complex mathematical structure in nature. As I've said, this kind of extraordinary fit of mathematical description and prediction to physical reality cannot be explained by trivial logical necessity. So what *does* explain it?

I've offered an explanation that appeals to mind: just as an intelligent civilization might build a structure that maps onto complex astronomical processes, so God created a world that maps onto a rich mathematical structure. But it seems you don't even want to concede that Wigner and Einstein were right to be amazed.

Justin: Let me again put my puzzlement toward your line of inquiry in the form of a question. What would a physical world *not* describable by some basic mathematical concepts even look like?

Perhaps you are more imaginative than I and can imagine an actual physical world resembling something like, oh, I don't know, those "worlds" found in the lithographic prints of Dutch artist M. C. Escher.

Randal: I do like M. C. Escher. In fact, I think I have an old Escher calendar somewhere.

Justin: Who doesn't?

Randal: But I'm not thinking about that here. I've already noted that every possible world would map onto some basic mathematical concepts. But the special theory of relativity is not a basic mathematical concept. We're dealing with an extraordinary degree of fit here. As I've said, that degree of rational, mathematical structure in nature is not surprising on theism but it is on atheism.

Justin: Well, that's not at all obvious. To be clear, I think you are right to appeal to a mind when thinking about the relationship between mathematics and the sciences, but I think you've got the direction of explanation backward.

I think the precision with which the predictions of Einstein's equations were confirmed is in large part because of the effort spent on creating various systems of mathematics capable of representing the physical world with increasingly impressive precision.

Randal: Well sure, mathematicians like Einstein worked hard at *discovering* the nature of the world by way of complex mathematical calculations that were confirmed a century later by way of empirical observation. But how is that a rebuttal to my argument?

Justin: But, Randal, he didn't just pull the math out of thin air. With scientific theories, we impose various systems of mathematics onto our prior accumulated observations and come up with elegant explanations that both fit the data and make predictions about future observations. Sometimes these predictions are rather counterintuitive. The relations may get very complex, but the basic idea here isn't that different from predicting the basic trajectory of your baseball while knowing the relevant variables.

Randal: Sure, but how is that supposed to provide a rebuttal to what I've argued? You're merely redescribing the very phenomenon you need to explain!

Justin: There looks to be no substantive explanatory role for God to play in this process, and I suspect that is part of the reason why she is largely absent from physics departments.

The argument here, while of no obvious relevance to the God question, does provide incredibly powerful evidence for the intelligence, conceptual clarity, and creativity of physicists and mathematicians.

Randal: Your quip that God does not provide an explanatory role in physics departments suggests that you haven't understood my argument. I'm not appealing to God as a *physical* explanation but rather as a *metaphysical* one. We're doing *philosophy* here, not science, so we shouldn't expect to find God as an explanation in physics departments.

Justin: My response didn't distinguish between physical and metaphysical explanations because I've argued that positing God here is unsuccessful on both counts.

Randal: Okay, but I've *never* appealed to God as a physical explanation so, unless you're just trying to get a rhetorical advantage, it simply isn't relevant to say that God is absent from the physics department. That said, we *do* agree, at least, on the great intelligence of physicists and mathematicians. (As the saying goes, be grateful for small mercies!)

But, as I've pointed out, these very physicists and mathematicians, folks like Einstein and Wigner, recognize that they are *discovering* the mathematical structure of the world, and they are left in awe of that structure. I've provided a philosophical explanation for that structure. Just as an archaeoastronomer would appeal to mind to explain the fit of physical structure to astronomical events and processes, so I've appealed to mind to explain the fit of mathematical structure to physical events and processes.

Justin: I see no explanatory reason to posit God as a response to these issues, and you see God as the best explanation for this correspondence between our mathematical concepts and the physical world. Here I think we end in yet another stalemate with respect to this argument.

Randal: So yet again I'm persuaded that I won, and you're persuaded that you won. This is starting to get predictable. Perhaps we should ask somebody to serve as a tiebreaker to decide which of us is right. How about I give my mom a call? We can both share our arguments and she can decide who wins.

Justin: That won't be necessary, Randal. I gave your mom a rundown of the arguments over a nice candlelit dinner last night. She found my arguments difficult to resist and now calls herself an atheist.

You left yourself wide open for that one.

Randal: Hah! My parents called me last night laughing that some weirdo came up to them at the mall food court yesterday trying to convince them that atheism was true. When my mom politely said she was *a theist* the guy got really excited, thinking she said *atheist*.

So that was you, eh? Good to know. But hey, don't look so disappointed. You've got one more try to convince me of something.

Chapter 7

EVOLUTION AND THE BIOLOGICAL ROLE OF PAIN

Justin: I suppose then that it is my turn yet again to offer up another argument in favor of atheism and against theism.

Randal: I think you're right! I hope you've got something really good to bring our meandering conversation to a memorable conclusion.

Justin: I hope I don't disappoint.

Randal: Yeah, and I hope you do. I want to win this one. So what you got?

PRELIMINARY COMMENTS ON GOD, EVIL, AND SUFFERING

Justin: There is one such argument (or family of arguments) that I suspect is familiar to nearly every person who has ever pondered the specific concept of God we have been struggling with throughout this exchange. These arguments, as with my other arguments, are seen as problems for theism. These problems come in many different logical structures and names, but they all appeal to some fact or facts about the existence of or nature of suffering in the actual world.

Randal: Ah, I was wondering when the venerable problems from evil and suffering would make an appearance. And let me say at the outset that this *is* a big problem for any theist. And while the intellectual side of the problem of evil and suffering is bad enough, from a personal perspective the *experience* of evil and suffering is far worse. Nothing can shake a person's belief in God like the shattering experience of deep pain, suffering, and loss.

Justin: Unfortunately, when it comes to the problem of our *experience* of pain and suffering, the atheist is no better off than the theist. That's true even if, as I'll attempt to argue, the atheist does enjoy a considerable advantage with respect to the intellectual problem.

Randal: Interesting. I agree that everybody suffers, if that's what you mean. At the same time, I do believe that theism has one significant advantage straight out of the gate in that it provides *hope for a final deliverance* from suffering that atheism doesn't offer. And that belief in a hopeful future in turn conveys psychological benefits that can help ameliorate the degree of suffering a person will endure.

Justin: While I agree that some religious versions of theism offer a final deliverance, that compensation hardly serves as a justification. Moreover, it's not clear to me that this is true in terms of the bare theism being discussed in this book. After all, theism does not entail that there would be any kind of life after death.

Though, admittedly, life after death is more probable on theism than on atheism.

Randal: No doubt. And you're right to point out that our relatively barebones definition of theism doesn't include life after death. But it does include God's maximal power and perfect goodness, and those attributes together provide a significant ground for hope. So whether or not one agrees with Immanuel Kant's famous claim that a just God would secure an afterlife where justice is satisfied, one can hopefully agree that, all things being equal, it is better for those who suffer that a maximally good and just being exists than not.

But by no means am I claiming this eliminates the problem. Either way, I admit that we theists do face a challenge here.

Justin: Oh, I see what you're saying, and I think I agree.

Randal: Awesome! Since we agree, how about we end the chapter right now on that high note of common accord?

Justin: And rob patient readers of the spectacle that is a theist dealing with variations on the age-old problem of suffering? I wouldn't dare!

Randal: Oh blarg!

EVOLUTION AND ATHEISM: A MATCH MADE IN HEAVEN?

Justin: Now, the specific argument that I want to press here for this last exchange is similar to my other arguments in that it seeks to draw out a particular set of facts that hold true in the actual world but that are better explained on the assumption that no God exists (as defined) than on the assumption that God does exist.

Randal: Sounds fine to me. Just let me buckle my seatbelt in preparation for the rocky road that lies ahead.

Okay, I'm ready to go. You may fire when ready!

Justin: This argument, inspired by the work of Paul Draper, centers around a few basic facts.

Randal: Excellent. Arguments are always better when they start with facts.

Justin: The first fact to which the argument appeals is the fact that evolution is the way by which the variety of living things on earth has come about. The second fact is about the relationships between pain and pleasure and the biological goals of survival and reproduction. Together, I think they provide a powerful argument for atheism.

Now, with regard to the issue of evolution, I'm not going to claim that our knowledge of evolution proves atheism, but I am going to claim that it serves as evidence that favors atheism over theism.

Randal: Since the reader can't see me, let the record reflect that my eyebrows are rising in incredulity.

Justin: Eyebrow movement noted.

Specifically, my first claim is that, when we abstract away from our knowledge of the evidence for evolution, evolution turns out to be much more expected on the atheistic hypothesis than on theism. As a result, our knowledge of evolution strongly favors atheism over theism.

See, given the fact of the existence of varied and complex life, if atheism is true evolution pretty much *must* be true because, according to what we know, there are no other viable options.

Randal: Let me flag my disagreement with this point. But finish your argument and I'll come back to my objection later. I don't want to derail you in the middle of your tactical assault.

Justin: Okay, that's fair. Now, where was I? Oh, yes; I remember.

So, what about on theism? Well, theism gives us a number of reasons to be surprised that evolution is true that simply don't exist on atheism. First of all, on theism, God could have brought about a variety of creatures in a number of different ways. So, if theism is true, then it's burdened with the fact that God just so happened to choose the one way available on atheism for bringing about complex and varied life: evolution. This is a stunning coincidence.

Secondly, evolution can only occur with massive amounts of suffering and death. It's important to appreciate the sheer scale of the suffering and death: millions of years' worth! It's also important to notice that this suffering and death is not just an accidental byproduct of evolution. Rather, it is intrinsic to the system. Given that theism posits a God with moral motivations, theism must say that there exists some justification for all this death and suffering. That is an additional detail that the theistic hypothesis is saddled with, whereas, on atheism, no further detail beyond the fact of evolution is necessary to explain the suffering and death. So that is an additional sense in which atheism enjoys an explanatory advantage over theism with regard to the scientific fact of evolution.

Randal: Okay, like I said, I want to start off and raise an objection. But, before I do, I'd like you to step back for a moment and say something more about how you are defining evolution, since different readers may have somewhat different concepts in mind.

Justin: Very true. It's certainly important that I get clear on exactly what is meant by *evolution*. Here though, I'm going defer to philosopher Paul Draper, the original defender of this argument, so that I don't have to do the work.

Randal: Paul Draper is here? Awesome! So where is he?

Justin: Found him! The relevant passage is from Draper's 1997 article, "Evolution and the Problem of Evil":

> By "evolution," I mean the conjunction of two theses.
>
> The first, which I will call "the genealogical thesis," asserts that evolution did in fact occur—complex life did evolve from relatively simple life. Specifically, it is the view that all multicellular organisms and all (relatively) complex unicellular organisms on earth (both present and past) are the (more or less) gradually modified descendants of a small number of relatively simple unicellular organisms.
>
> The second thesis, which I will call "the genetic thesis," addresses the issue of how evolution occurred. It states that all evolutionary change in populations of complex organisms

either is or is the result of trans-generational genetic change (or, to be more precise, trans-generational change in nucleic acids).[1]

It's important, I think, to notice that Draper is also careful to distinguish that last claim from the much more specific claim that purely unguided (Darwinian) natural selection operating on random mutations is the primary driver of evolutionary change.

Randal: And why is this distinction important?

Justin: Well, it's because an evidential argument from evolution against theism that assumed from the start that the primary driver of evolutionary change was purely unguided natural selection (rather than guided selection) acting on random mutation (rather than guided mutation) would be, in a sense, begging the question against the theist who believes that, at the fundamental level, the mutations and selection are indeed guided.

Randal: Fair enough. I actually don't think that is an issue with using the concept of random mutation, so long as one recognizes that science doesn't deal with metaphysical appeals *to* God or denials *of* God. In my view, any scientific appeal to randomness is a separate topic from the providential involvement of any deity in those random processes, since science simply doesn't address theological or supernatural causes. But this point is a potential rabbit trail, so I'm happy to drop it.

Justin: I see your point. Well, before I move to the second half of my argument regarding the relationships between pain, pleasure, survival, and reproduction, did you have any objection to the first half on evolution?

Randal: Hmm, yeah, perhaps this is when I should raise the concern I noted above.

Justin: Ah, yes. I almost forgot. So what was your concern?

ATHEISTIC ALTERNATIVES TO EVOLUTION?

Randal: You said that if atheism is true then "evolution pretty much *must* be true because, according to what we know, there are no other viable options." And thus, so you said, if it should turn out that theism is true it would be a "stunning coincidence" that life should have originated through the one way consistent with atheism.

Here's where I must lodge my disagreement. Just because you are not *aware* of any other explanations for the origin of species consistent with atheism, it doesn't follow that there *are* no other options.

Justin: That's a good point. Notice though, that I was careful to cast this argument in epistemic terms. Given the complete lack of viable alternatives, it's highly probable that, if atheism is true, evolution must also be true because we observe the fact that a variety of life does indeed exist.

Randal: Interesting. But alas, I don't think that follows at all. The history of science is a history of theories at one time confidently held and supported by an abundance of evidence but later overturned. So how do you know that there will not be a completely different theory in fifty years to explain biological diversity?

Justin: Yes, that is of course possible, and, if the facts were to change, then the argument would have to take on that new information and adjust accordingly. But Randal, this is the case with *all* evidential arguments on *all* sides of *any* debate that appeal to the current state of acquired knowledge.

From where I stand, this is not so much an objection as it is a reminder to us both of the limits of evidential inferences in general.

Randal: No, it's an objection. You see, I'm not merely making a general observation about the broadly qualified nature of evidential inferences. Rather, I'm pointing to a past *track record* of failed scientific theories as justification for skepticism that a current scientific theory will remain the definitive, correct theory. And note, by the way, that this argument precisely parallels your appeal to an (alleged) track record of past failed theological theories as grounds to justify rejecting my theistic explanation of mathematical structure in nature.

Perhaps I can unpack my point with an illustration. Imagine that you and I are driving a twisty road to a new city. I ask you, "When will we get there?" and you reply, "Just around that next bend!" But as we turn the bend we find no city. Later I ask again, "When will we get there?" and again you reply, "Just around that next bend!" And doggone it, once again you're wrong! This same scenario then plays out several more times. The tenth time you tell me the city is just around the next bend, I'll have a strong undercutting defeater to your testimony. In other words, while you still *could* be right, given your past track record the rational thing to do is withhold belief.

That illustration provides a fitting analogue for our current state of knowledge regarding scientific theories. Just as your reports of the approaching city continue to be falsified in the analogy, so it is with those who declare that a particular scientific theory has provided the definitive account of a given subject matter. Theories keep getting falsified, radically revised, and just plain abandoned.

And, just to be clear, my point is not that evolution or any other theory *will* be falsified. Nor is it even that any particular theory will *probably* be falsified. Just as the city could be around the next bend so this could be the definitively correct theory. Rather, the point is simply that, from our present standpoint, *we simply lack knowledge to render an informed judgment on the question.* So, just as I should withhold assent the next time you claim that the city really is around the next corner, given the past track record of scientific theory failure (falsification, abandonment, etc.), we ought to withhold assent in the final correctness of neo-Darwinian evolution. And that, in turn, means that your claim that it is highly probable that evolution will be true if atheism is true is simply unjustified.

Justin: But Randal, my argument does *not* assume that evolution will never be falsified. It simply says, given the current state of information, this is what follows. Are you saying that the mere possibility of any scientific consensus being falsified in the future means that we cannot make evidential arguments with "highly probable" conclusions at all?

Randal: My objection isn't based on the assumption that you believe evolution will never be falsified. Rather, it's based on the claim that, given the past history of theory failure, you lack the ground to make any probable judgments since you simply cannot project on the future course of scientific advance in the coming decades and centuries. Just as a past history of failed reports that the city is around the next bend undermines the present testimonial report that the city is around the next bend, so the past history of scientific theory change on an issue like biological origins undermines the ground to believe that a neo-Darwinian evolutionary account will probably never be replaced or radically revised.

At this point, Robert Crease and Charles Mann provide a salutary warning when they recount the confident attitude of many physicists at the end of the nineteenth century. According to Crease and Mann, at that time many scientists

> believed that all of physics was already known and that future generations of scientists would only buff and polish the insights of the past. Indeed, the certainty with which many physical scientists of the 1880s thought they had the fundamental puzzles nailed down is today a source of puzzlement to scholars. At Harvard University, for instance, the then-head of the physics department, John Trowbridge, felt compelled to warn bright graduate students away from physics. The essential business of the science is finished, he told them.[2]

Then Albert Einstein appeared on the scene and the rest is history.

Who knows what Einstein might appear tomorrow in physics, geology, or biology to offer astounding new insights that will shake solid paradigms to their foundations? So the simple lesson is that your inference outstrips the evidence you have for it. And this means that you are simply not justified in your claim that evolution will be true if atheism is true.

Justin: I must admit to being confused by your comments here. This has nothing to do with any future expectations, Randal. Of course our current theoretical framework may be overturned in the future, but that doesn't disallow us from talking about what follows from our best and most current theories.

Currently, the best explanation for the diversity of life is evolution. Now, if we conditionalize on *that fact* and *if* atheism is true, it follows that evolution practically had to be true. And again that is informed by the current state of knowledge and may change. This is true regardless of past changes in scientific consensus. So, contrary to what you've said, my claim here is *not to be equated with* the claim that it is highly probable that evolution will never be overturned for another theory.

Randal: No, no, no. Just because you now believe x is a fact it doesn't follow that x *practically had to be true.* Alas, I fear we're going in circles here. Perhaps I should shift my point of critique. The fact is that there are many theories for the origin of the diversity of life on earth that *are* consistent with atheism, including presently defunct theories like Lamarckianism, spontaneous generation, and panspermia, as well as countless theories not yet imagined. So I see no rigid connection as you apparently do between the current dominance of neo-Darwinian evolution and the possible truth of atheism.

That said, I don't want to derail your argument any further. Feel free to proceed when ready.

Justin: Before I move on, I do want to note that I mentioned a lack of *plausible* alternatives on *atheism* for explaining the *diversity of life.* Special creation is inapplicable for that reason. As for the others, they either are attempts to explain the *origin* rather than the *diversity* of life, or they lack a plausible mechanism.

Randal: Wait a minute. Spontaneous generation is *not* the same thing as special creation nor does it require theism. Moreover, Lamarckianism explicitly explains diversity and panspermia readily could as well. And as I said, the lack of a current plausible alternative does not warrant the conclusion that there will be no plausible alternative.

Justin: Yeah, I think I'm going to move on to the latter half of the argument now.

Randal: By all means.

NEW AND IMPROVED COMPETITORS

Justin: For the second half of this chapter, I want to treat the biological fact of evolution (from the first half of this chapter) as an add-on to theism and to atheism. When we add evolution to each of these hypotheses, we get two "extended hypotheses." Let's call these extended hypotheses "theistic evolution" and "atheistic evolution," the *new and improved* competitors.

Now I want to take these extended hypotheses and compare them as to their ability to explain some interesting facts about the experience of pain and pleasure. In doing so, we will discover the *second* evidential boost for atheism over theism in this chapter (evolution itself was the first). So, what is this new evidence I wish to consider?

Randal: You took the words right out of my mouth! What evidence, pray tell?

Justin: Okay, so, when it comes to the experience of pain (and pleasure), much of it that happens in the world is clearly systematically connected to the biological goals of survival and reproduction.[3]

Randal: Slow down buddy. You're tossing out a lot of highfalutin' concepts here. I think some further explanation will be helpful.

Justin: Guilty as charged. I suppose an example might help. Philosopher Paul Draper uses the example of how a warm fire on a cold night is something we typically find pleasurable, while lying naked in a snow bank is something we typically find painful. He notes that this is because maintaining a constant and physiologically safe body temperature increases the chances that the organism will survive and reproduce. The biological usefulness of pain perception for an organism's survival becomes even clearer when we see how difficult it can be for those who live completely without pain to stay alive or to avoid serious injury. Of course, pleasure too is often biologically useful. For example, the pleasure we experience during sex increases our chances of engaging in sexual activity and that increases our chances of reproducing.

Randal: I'd like to pause at the point where you say the reason folks don't like chillin' in a snow bank is because the maintenance of a safe body temperature increases the chances that they will survive and reproduce. It might help if I give voice to a skeptic. This skeptic happens to be a twenty-year-old snowboarder named Brody who has some familiarity with the practice. So Brody, what do you think about Justin's claim?

Brody: *Dude, the guy is nuts! The reason I don't lie naked in snow banks is because it's painful dude, not because I want to have a brat some day! And believe me bro, I've tried the snow bank plunge. It* ain't *fun.*

Randal: Thanks for sharing your thoughts, Brody.

So Justin, what would you say to my incredulous snowboarding friend who balks at your explanation for his behavior?

Justin: Well, first I'd caution Brody against pulling his bleached tips out over this. Notice that even if Brody as an individual has no interest in having a brat, he still has an interest in the biological goal of surviving. But, really, that's beside the point. It is in fact the case that the bodily systems that cause his experience of pain and pleasure are oriented toward the biological goals of survival and reproduction. He may not intellectually grasp the biological importance of maintaining a constant and safe body temperature, but that doesn't mean that these systems are not the reasons for his experiencing pain.

Of course, there is another interesting fact about pain and pleasure: not *all* pain/pleasure is biologically useful. For example, imagine the horrible pain experienced by the family who eventually perishes in a house fire, or the excruciating pain experienced by those with horrible terminal illnesses. Those examples of pain fail to be biologically useful because they do not contribute to biological goals. Pleasure can fail to be biologically useful as well. Consider the pleasure experienced every time the drug addict feeds his crippling addiction.

If *atheistic evolution* is true, then we can expect purely natural and blind (Darwinian) processes to be responsible for the existence of pain and pleasure in the world. Atheistic evolution makes it likely that humans, if they exist, will be the goal-oriented organic systems that they actually are. Humans will be composed of parts that are systematically oriented toward biological goals like survival and/or reproduction. If pain and pleasure do exist, we'd expect that they too are systematically oriented toward those biological goals.

But with theistic evolution things would look very different. On theistic evolution, these facts would be rather surprising.

Randal: Of course, I'm going to ask you why you think these facts would be surprising on theistic evolution. So, um, why do you think that?

Justin: First, if theistic evolution is true, pain and pleasure only exist because God has indirectly guided (or permitted) blind processes to fashion bodies with that capacity. God, being morally perfect and unburdened by the very biological laws over which she is sovereign, wouldn't permit pain (even biologically useful pain) without powerful *moral* reasons. A mere biological reason wouldn't suffice because an omnipotent God is capable of creating humans without biologically useful pain or pleasure. Therefore, we have much more reason to be *surprised* that pain and pleasure systematically contribute to biological goals in this way on theism than we do on atheism.

Randal: God would only create a diversity of species through evolutionary means if doing so was consistent with his perfect moral nature. So if one has independent reasons to believe God exists, reasons such as I've provided, *and* if one believes an evolutionary account of biological diversity is correct, then it follows that the biological reasons for pain and pleasure are consistent with God's moral nature.

What's so surprising about that?

Justin: Nothing in my argument should be interpreted as my claiming that theism is inconsistent with there being some biological reasons for some pain and pleasure. Moreover, simply noting that if theism were true, then all suffering must be consistent with God's nature (morally justified in some way) does nothing to address the question of whether the evidence I've mentioned about the systematic yet blind role pain plays with respect to the biological goals of survival and reproduction supports theism or atheism.

So, remember how I mentioned that much of pain and pleasure fails to be biologically useful?

Randal: Yes, yes, I do.

Justin: Well, on atheistic evolution, the processes at work are wholly blind, imperfect, and incapable of fine-tuning experiences of pain and pleasure so that they only occur when biologically useful. On theism, however, these pain receptors need not be so blind to the circumstances. On theism, God could fine-tune pain receptors to deliver only a painful sensation when it would contribute to the biological goals of the organism.

It's often asserted that God is capable of fine-tuning the cosmological constants for the existence of life, but the issue of God's suspicious failure to fine-tune pain receptors is rarely ever discussed.

In the actual world, the family trapped in the burning house *will* experience the hell of the heat. The man on his deathbed *will* experience the hell of being slowly eaten by his infection. The torture victim *will* feel every excruciating rip of pain before his captors eventually end his life.

These examples of pain are as real and deeply felt as they are useless with respect to biological goals.

These examples are also much easier to explain on atheism, whereas on theism we have to assume that in every case there also happens to be moral justifications. That's a huge detail that the theist must saddle himself with. The atheist, on the other hand, is entirely unsurprised that our pain receptors so clearly seem crafted by an indifferent and blind process rather than a morally perfect, omniscient God.

CONSCIOUSNESS AND MATERIAL CREATION: WHICH IS MORE SURPRISING?

Randal: Well, I don't think that's much for the theist to saddle himself with. After all, if the meticulously provident deity of classical theism exists, then the moral justification for all evils that occur follows naturally. Your reasoning is like a person saying "But if God exists then he created planets *and* nebulae *and* stars *and* black holes! That's a huge detail that the theist must saddle himself with." No, no, it isn't. If God exists then it follows naturally that he created all those things. And if God exists then it follows naturally that every evil has a moral justification.

I must say that this line of argument strikes me as ironic given how extraordinary it is that pain, and conscious states in general, should exist at all within an atheistic universe. Consider, according to the theist consciousness is basic, for God is himself a disembodied mind that brings both matter and finite embodied minds into existence. Consequently, it is hardly surprising that God should produce a universe with conscious minds. By contrast, on atheism the emergence of consciousness is completely unexpected and inexplicable. So as I said, it seems rather ironic that you're appealing to the fact of pain to support atheism when that fact entails the more general fact of consciousness, which is already extremely surprising on atheism but not on theism.

Justin: Let me first agree that, when it comes to conscious states, I too find them less likely to arise on atheism than on theism because theism entails God's conscious states. But admitting this is not at all inconsistent with my argument. There is nothing improper about identifying a general statement that supports one hypothesis while many of its known details lend strong support to an entirely different, incompatible hypothesis.

I tend to see your worry regarding conscious states and their ability to arise on atheism as a parallel to an argument in the opposite direction. If, as you say, conscious states are basic on theism, then for that and other reasons, it is the physical that is unexpected and inexplicable on theism. It's not at all obvious to me that these concerns do anything other than cancel each other out.

Randal: I'm glad you agree that the existence of consciousness is more surprising on atheism than on theism. But I don't agree that the theist faces a comparable problem as regards the alleged surprising existence of matter. To argue your case, you need to provide some basis to believe that if God creates he is more likely to actualize nonphysical or immaterial substances than physical or material ones. But how would you justify that claim?

Justin: Well, no, that's not necessary. See, I think the problem goes *further* back than that. One of the most basic questions to ask is whether or not God, if she existed, would create *anything* in the first place. I'm certainly not the first person to point out that it's not remotely obvious why God would ever choose to create any finite thing outside of her morally and ontologically perfect self. The second and equally strange assumption that God, if she ever actually chose to create, would create physical stuff rather than "nonphysical" stuff is also far from obvious.

Randal: As I already noted earlier in this conversation, God wouldn't create out of need.

Justin: I can agree with that.

Randal: But that is quite different from claiming God would likely not create at all, for one can create for many reasons other than need. For example, many artists bring their artistic works into being because it is of their very nature to be artists. And many theists have thought about God in an analogous sense, not that God creates out of need but rather out of the superabundant creativity of his very nature.

Justin: On the one hand, if you want to define God as creative *by definition* (as an artist is), you've immediately contradicted your above claim that creation was *not* done out of necessity. On the other, if

God's creation act was a free act, then we're left to make sense of God's bizarre intentional decision to dilute the overall perfection of the most pure and perfect state of affairs that has ever existed, which is God's existing alone. If God exists, this possible world will forever be *stained* by her decision to bring about the finite, limited, and imperfect entities.

Randal: I didn't say God necessarily creates, though interestingly many theologians (both inside and outside the Judeo-Christian tradition) *have* considered creation to be a necessary expression of God's nature. And that's precisely opposite to your supposition that God wouldn't create. As for the mainstream Christian perspective, on that view creation is a natural but not necessary expression of God's nature.

And I reject your suggestion that the possible world in which God alone exists is somehow greater than the possible worlds in which God exists with a creation. I see nothing to support that claim. Indeed, your logic would suggest that God would be unable to bring any creation into existence because the creation of anything other than God would entail a dilution of overall goodness. But this claim flatly contradicts the doctrine of omnipotence.

Justin: I disagree. This doesn't contradict omnipotence because omnipotence doesn't entail the possibility of doing something contrary to one's essential moral nature. If omnipotence *did* entail such a thing, then God's *inability* to do an *evil* act would equally count against her omnipotence.

Randal: And I see zero reason to think the very act of creation would violate God's moral nature.

But look, I don't want my ain't-consciousness-surprising-on-atheism rejoinder to obscure your main point here. So let's do a quick review. If I understand you correctly, you're saying that if atheism were true we would expect a crude fit between pain and the biological benefits of that pain. But if theism were true we would expect a more precise fit, since God would not want his creatures to experience unnecessary pain. Since the fit we do in fact find in nature is crude rather than precise, this favors atheism over theism. Is that correct?

Justin: I'm saying that, if theism were true, we have more reason to think that pain and pleasure wouldn't just behave like other biological mechanisms than we would on atheism. This is because of the moral significance that pain and pleasure can have on our lives.

If there is to be pain and pleasure on theism, we'd have more reason to expect them to be aimed at *moral* goals rather than *biological* goals. We'd rightly be surprised when we witness the excruciating pain of the family as they slowly die in a house fire, as God could easily "turn off" such sensations once they are not contributing to the biological goal of survival. Theism requires that all such biologically unnecessary suffering that results from poorly tuned pain receptors is connected to some moral justification. But theism is then left with explaining why moral justifications so map onto pain and pleasure in a way that perfectly resembles the systematic goal-directedness toward biological goals that we'd expect on purely Darwinian, unguided evolution.

GOD'S HIDDEN REASONS?

Randal: Tell me Justin, how do you think God should've done it? In other words, how would the world have to look for your objection to be satisfied?

Justin: The moral significance that pain and pleasure have in terms of the ability for moral agents to have good lives and affect the lives of others gives us strong reason to expect that, on theism, the bodily subsystems that produce pain and pleasure should be different from other subsystems. God could have guided evolution such that the relationship between pain and our bodies would be so that we only felt pain when, say, doing something wrong, rather than as a result of blind biological systems. The family trapped in the house fire experiencing excruciating pain before their eventual death makes more sense on the indifference entailed by Darwinian atheistic evolution than on the guiding hand of God posited by theistic evolution.

Basically, on theism, we have more reason to expect the doomed family *not* to experience pain.

Randal: Thanks for unpacking that a bit more. I must admit that while I definitely feel the emotional appeal of the problem of evil, I've always been deeply skeptical of the way that skeptics have relatively confident beliefs about how an infinitely knowledgeable, benevolent, and wise being should run things.

Justin: Hmm. Okay, but are you equally skeptical when theists such as yourself make claims about how an infinitely knowledgeable, benevolent, and wise being should run things? Because nearly every argument that we've so far discussed on both sides includes claims about what we should expect from such a hypothesis.

Randal: No, I'm not equally skeptical about the theist. You see, I'm seeking to do two things in our conversation. First, on the offensive, I'm providing positive arguments for the existence of God. Second, on the defensive, I'm providing objections, those undercutting and rebutting defeaters, to your arguments against the existence of God. On the defensive front, my task is to show that theism is perfectly consistent with the evidence you provide. So until you provide independent reasons for me to question my assumptions about God, I'll be happy to retain them. Moreover, those who find them persuasive are rational to adopt them.

I suspect we can all envision instances where, contrary to all expectation, extraordinary goods were borne of the most ignoble circumstances. If one considers the prospect that God is providentially active in the world, one will have grounds to view the evils that occur, as horrible as they may be in themselves, nonetheless as explicable within a larger economy in which God uses those evils to give rise to greater goods. And the fact that we cannot currently see what those goods are is not an adequate reason to think they don't exist.

Justin: I fully agree that if one is committed to belief in God, they will interpret such evils or sufferings as justified in some way. Often such persons will appeal to what they think of as a greater good and then claim (with varying degrees of success) that the suffering in question was necessary in order for God to obtain that greater good or, perhaps, to avoid some equally bad or worse instance of suffering. If theism is true, then it must be that all sufferings (or evils) that *actually* occur are morally best all-things-considered. Any failure to locate God's possible justifications for permitting the worst horrors in the world is merely the fault of our epistemic limitations.

Randal: I couldn't have said it better myself! Well, maybe I could have, but that was still darn good, except for the "best-all-things-considered" description.

Justin: But I'm not particularly interested in how a committed theist might seek to explain the suffering. Rather, I'm interested in the separate issue of whether or not the facts to which I've so far referred constitute evidence against theism. But this brings up an interesting point. As an aside, consider what follows from this about the following horrors that have actually happened.

> *If* theism is true, the Holocaust was morally best, all things considered (even if we may not know God's morally good reasons for permitting this).
>
> *If* theism is true, it is routinely best, all things considered, for a parent to kill their child (even if we may not know God's morally good reasons for permitting this).
>
> *If* theism is true, it is morally best, all things considered, for Private Killum to torture, kill, and mutilate the Nazi POW (even if we may not know God's morally good reasons for permitting this).

The list could go on and on for all actual horrors in the world. My worry is that theists are in a bit of a moral bind here. If theism is true and horrors are often morally best all things considered, it would seem that our moral *intuitions* about what is a good act or state of affairs are *radically* confused.

Randal: I'm glad to see you haven't forgotten my Private Killum example. However, I'm not sure what you mean by saying it is *morally best* for these evils to occur.

Justin: Ah, allow me to explain. When I say that some actual event is morally best, all things considered, on theism, I am referring to the fact that, if theism is true, God has providentially picked a world to create and has chosen according to her infinite wisdom (and for reasons unavailable to us) to fill it with the happenings that she has. We must assume that her reasons for choosing *these* events (rather than some other, tamer happenings) to occur are among the best possible kinds of moral reasons.

God could have prevented the Holocaust but she didn't. We must infer then that, if God exists, the Holocaust was morally necessary for some unknown reason. A lesser evil wouldn't have been sufficient to achieve whatever mysterious moral goal God was after. The Holocaust, then, was morally best all things considered.

Randal: I have two points by way of reply. First, the fact that God has morally sufficient reasons for allowing evil has *absolutely no implications* for our moral intuitions. It does not follow that our moral intuitions are, as you say, "radically confused." An evil act is, in itself, still an evil act, even if God still has a morally sufficient reason to allow it to occur.

Justin: Yeah, I don't think that helps. If theists have in their background knowledge the fact that, for example, murders and rapes actually happen every day all around the world and so must have been morally best, all things considered (even though we may not know *why* they are morally best), it will not be at all obvious to them whether or not to intervene on behalf of the next victim they see.

Randal: The fact that you keep using the term "morally best" to refer to actions that are themselves morally heinous has the whiff of a rhetorical gambit. But I fear that only perpetuates confusion. If a moral agent has morally sufficient reasons to allow an evil event to occur, that allowance does not thereby transmute the evil into something good, let alone something morally best. I said it before and I'll say it again: the act itself is still an evil even though it was allowed for a greater good.

Justin: I've not claimed that divine allowance makes some evil event into a morally good one. When I say something is morally best in this context, I mean it was the best or one of the best options available, such that, if we could see it from a God's eye view, it would be like the pain experienced by the child receiving a flu shot—best when all things are being considered.

Randal: Hey, I need to take on your suggestion that an account of God's allowing evil for greater good would undermine a basis for moral action. That seems to me to be patently false. Our ground for moral action is constituted by the moral good and our specific moral obligations and callings to live in accord with it, and I've presented a theistic case for both. In short, we have a moral obligation to prevent evil where possible, even as we know that God has a morally sufficient reason to allow the evils we fail to prevent.

I also want to come back to your statement that the evils that

God allows are somehow morally *best* for his purposes. This simply doesn't follow. All that follows is that God has morally sufficient reasons to allow the evils that do occur. There could be an *infinite* number of feasible worlds that God could choose to actualize that are consistent with his moral nature and have a commensurate distribution of goods and evils to the world God in fact created.

Justin: This is why I specifically refer to the *actual* world context in which these *actual* events occur with the phrase "all things considered."

I've argued that, on theism, all actual horrible events/actions are, to be more precise, morally best, or at least among the morally best live options in our actual world. I've argued that this undermines our ability to make moral decisions. You've disagreed and again mentioned your theistic explanations of morality from earlier.

Randal: Okay, but *morally best* is not the same thing as *among the morally best live options.* My primary issue is with the former description rather than the latter one.

Justin: The problem is that it's not at all obvious how you think this solves anything.

I imagine you use background information regarding likely causes and outcomes of events when making moral choices, to best inform your efforts toward what you see as your obligations.

Now, if you know that murders actually occur with a high frequency, then you have an overwhelming amount of background information that says that, very frequently in the actual world, murders are among the best moral options for God to achieve her ends.

Randal: No, Justin, my moral judgment that murder is wrong is not based primarily on background information regarding the likely causes and outcomes of murder. Rather, as I pointed out in our discussion of moral perception, it's rooted in an immediate perceptual grasp of the wrongness of the action, a grasp that can subsequently be strengthened by discursive reasoning. And that intuition or immediate perception provides the basis for our grasp of moral value and obligation.

And God allows murders because God has morally sufficient reasons to do so. That doesn't change my moral obligation to prevent murder where possible. Think again of John Rabe, called to protect the innocent in Nanjing.

Justin: Okay, but our intuitions are often *shaped* by past moral experiences. These are experiences in our background information. My only point is that you might not *understand* what God's exact reasons are for these tragedies but your background information tells you that very, very often they do, in fact, exist if theism is true. To the theist who rationally incorporates this rich amount of background information into their decision-making, it will not be at all obvious to them whether or not to intervene if given the opportunity to stop a murder.

Randal: Once again for good measure: our moral duty is to prevent evil while knowing that God has a morally sufficient reason to allow the evil we fail to prevent.

And as for the problem of evil you've presented, the question is whether the person open to the arguments I've presented for theism should think you've provided a good reason to think God doesn't exist.

Justin: I disagree. I began this chapter by promising to offer evidence which *favors* atheism over theism. Now, everybody has different starting points, and of course they may have other arguments to consider (like your pro-theism arguments), and perhaps they'll end their investigation on the theistic side of the fence with you.

Randal: Sounds good to me. The grass is definitely greener over here.

Justin: I'm sure you think that. My only point is that that's a separate question from whether the information I'm offering up in this chapter counts as evidence favoring atheism over theism.

Randal: My point here is that your argument is of negligible impact for a person who is already a theist, since they readily assimilate the evils of the world into their overarching providential framework.

Justin: But, Randal, this is trivial if their ad hoc assimilation strategies are poor or inductively confused. After all, I've never claimed that all theists should find these arguments compelling.

Moreover, I could make the same trivial point against all the arguments you've presented in this book. I'm not interested in winning converts per se. I'm interested in what hypothesis the evidence favors.

Randal: Hold up there, kemosabe; I'm not talking about people who exhibit "ad hoc assimilation strategies." One of my primary concerns with this attempt to appeal to evil as evidence against God involves the issue of cognitive limitations. In my view, you are simply not in a position to opine on the kinds of reasons God could have to allow the evils that do occur. To object to God's existence based on the very limited experience we have of the world is equivalent to rejecting the novel of a Nobel Prize–winning author after reading the first page. Like the reader of that book, your selection sample is too limited. You're simply not in a position to draw an informed judgment.

Justin: There needs to be a careful distinction drawn out here. You claim that, because of the limited experience and knowledge of humans compared to God, we cannot rationally say that it is *unlikely* that God has some justifying reason for arranging things in such a way as the argument highlights. Now, if that was the argument, I'd probably agree with you.

Randal: Awesome.

Justin: It's not.

Randal: Aww, nuts.

Justin: It is essential, I think, to understand that this argument is *comparative* and centers around the explanatory merits of two distinct metaphysical theses. If, according to atheism in conjunction with blind, Darwinian evolution, the relevant observations to which I've drawn attention are likely, then this view has a certain degree of explanatory power. If, on theism, our knowledge in relation to God's has us skeptical of our ability to put any likelihood estimations on theism's ability to yield the relevant data, then theism scores poorly (relative to atheism) with respect to explaining the relevant data. At the very least then, the observational data regarding pain and suffering favors atheism.

Randal: Well, I've argued that Darwinian evolution doesn't favor atheism, since there are many theoretical possibilities to account for the origin of species on an atheistic view. So I don't think atheism has any advantage here.

Justin: You're certainly welcome to argue that.

Randal: And for that I am thankful!

Justin: But it's important to note that your conclusion that Darwinian evolution doesn't favor atheism does *not* logically follow from merely pointing out other theoretical *possibilities* on atheism. Besides, that was only the first half of the argument.

Randal: So here's the big question: should we expect this kind of world if theism is true? While I concede that a superficial reflection might say *no*, I think a deeper reflection will say *yes*. Time and again we find the truth in the wisdom that high reward only comes with high investment. God could have set us in a cosmic nursery where the biggest suffering is a stubbed toe. Or he could have hooked us all up to pleasure machines, the ultimate matrix.

Justin: To be honest, pleasure machines sound pretty sexy.

Randal: Hmm, sorry to disappoint you. But life is about far more than pleasure. It's about becoming people of virtue, *good* people.

And from that perspective, it isn't nearly as surprising that God put us in a world of undeniably great suffering, since this is also a world tuned for soul-making. On the other side of that dark night of the soul there is also inestimable reward in the attainment of courage, selflessness, compassion, and love. Those are the goods that God brings about through this veil of tears. And I'm content to defer to divine wisdom that those great goods give redemptive meaning to the suffering of the world.

INTO THE ICY DEPTHS OF GOD'S HIDDEN REASONS

Justin: At least with regard to the two main arguments I've presented in this chapter, evolution and the relationship between biological goals and pain, it isn't at all obvious that soul-making has anything substantive to add to theism's ability to explain any of it.

But now to a disturbing trend I've noticed repeatedly throughout this entire exchange, which was most clearly on display in your most recent comments. On the one hand, you boldly claim that we finite humans are "simply not in a position to opine on the kinds of reasons God could have to allow the evils that do occur."

Randal: That's right.

Justin: And yet, now you're doing just that by claiming that the goodness of soul-making is, in fact, one of the reasons that God allows evil to occur. What gives, Randal?

Randal: What gives? *What gives?* I'll tell you what gives!

In the passage you just quoted, I was not intending to claim that we can't have *any* knowledge about the reasons God might have to allow evil to occur. Indeed, it is part and parcel of the Christian tradition to claim we *do* have at least some knowledge in this area. See, for example, biblical passages such as Romans 5:3–5 and James 1:2–4. Rather, my intent was to claim that we don't have a comprehensive grasp of all the kinds of reasons God would have. In other words, the soul-making justifications cited in the two biblical passages I just referenced are the tip of what could be a very large iceberg.

Justin: Okay, I see.

However, there remains a problem with this response. If we have no idea whether or not the moral reasons represented in the "tip" of the proverbial iceberg are even roughly representative of the iceberg as a whole (and if we have no idea how *big* the *known* tip is compared to the *unknown* bulk of the berg), then we are in no position to make judgments regarding the likelihood of there being *contra*-soul-making concerns in the *unknown* bulk of the iceberg that cancel out the soul-making concerns you've brought up as represented in the "known" tip of the iceberg.

How's that for a run-on sentence?

Randal: Pretty impressive, actually!

Justin: When mystery is theism's greatest resource, explanations are its biggest weakness.

Randal: Oh wow, nice line. Seriously man, you could market that on merchandise at secular humanist conventions!

However, I must say there is some irony in all this. While you don't have much sympathy with the soul-making reasons God might have for allowing evil, you are quick to speculate on the possibility of additional so-called *contra-soul-making concerns*. What reason do you have to think that the perfect God would include these contra-soul-making reasons (whatever those may be) in his big iceberg of reasons for allowing evil?

Justin: The iceberg analogy is being used to illustrate the difference between the total moral reasons God, if she were to exist, would have available to her compared to the total number of moral reasons we, with our limited intellect, can plausibly see.

For all we know, the unseen bulk of the berg of reasons could be much larger than the portion we know of and might contain a myriad of reasons completely inconceivable to us. If God exists and what you say about our ignorance compared to God is true, then at the end of the day, we're simply not in a position to place any expectations on God's actions.

Randal: Um, I disagree. But go on.

Justin: But, Randal, for any reason on which you speculate in order to excuse God's poor fit with some horror in the world, there is always the fact that, for all we know, this reason is massively outweighed by unknown reasons (unknown to us but known to God) hiding below the surface that point in the exact opposite direction. Appealing to unknowns helps nobody because they cancel each other out.

The lesson here I think is that, once we say that we're not in a position to make judgment calls about the kinds of things God is likely to permit to occur on account of all the unknowns, we also rob ourselves of being in a position to make informed judgments that our favorite theodicy is not also outweighed by other reasons within that unknown-to-us section of God's epistemic iceberg.

Nevertheless, if we're comparing two hypotheses as to their ability to *explain* some set of data, a mystery-heavy hypothesis will perform poorly relative to most of its possible rivals. Compared to the ever-deepening mystery that is the theistic hypothesis, the indifference of atheism has a relatively easy time explaining the issues discussed in this chapter.[4]

Randal: For starters, I never endorsed your claim that "we're not in a position to make judgment calls about the kinds of things God is likely to permit. . . ." Quite the opposite, in fact. As I've pointed out, we have access to many of God's reasons, just not all of them. Moreover, since God is maximally good, we have excellent grounds to believe that whatever reasons he has for allowing evil are consistent with the desire that the maximum number of his creatures possible achieves a state of shalom (that is, wellness or flourishing).

To drive the point home I'm going to return to something you said earlier in this chapter, during our exchange on evolution. To recap, I raised the prospect that evolution could be overturned by a new scientific theory in the future. And you replied like this: "But

Randal, this is the case with *all* evidential arguments on *all* sides of *any* debate that appeal to the current state of acquired knowledge."

I didn't think that response worked in that context, and I explained why. But I *do* think it works here. The fact is that there is no reason at all to believe God is motivated by what you call contra-soul-making concerns, and so we can safely set that skeptical scenario aside.

Problem solved.

Justin: Eh, not so fast.

You've argued that, if God exists, we have access to *some* of her reasons. But, more importantly, you've also compared God's knowledge (and our access to it) to an iceberg. We can see the portion above water, but not the rest. In fact, we have no idea *how big* the submerged portion is so we also have no idea if the part we see is even roughly representative of the iceberg as a whole. For all we know, it could be massive down there.

Randal: No doubt.

Justin: So, with God's moral reasons, we see some of them, yes. But we don't know if the reasons we *do* see are even roughly representative of the *total reasons* that exist (only God knows them all).

The entire point of bringing this up is so that you can argue that we are *not* in a position to make likelihood inferences about the total moral reasons for which God might act *from* the moral reasons we can see. That is, *unless* we have good reason to think the moral reasons we see are representative of the whole of moral reasons available to God.

What follows then is that we are *not* in a position to say that there probably do not exist any contra-soul-making moral reasons. This is because we shouldn't expect to know about or "see" them even if they *did* exist. But if that is true, then we are also in no position to say that the posited soul-making reason you've given isn't cancelled out by these other possibly existing contra-soul-making moral reasons.

So, we're left yet again with theism being explanatorily blind when it comes to the facts about suffering (pain, evolution, etc.) that we observe in the world.

Randal: Explanatorily *blind?* I can see you're not pulling your punches here. Fair enough. If you want to play rough, we can both finish this book with some bumps and bruises!

So here's the essence of your proposed skeptical concern: while the theist purports to know some reasons why God allows evil, we can't claim to know that these reasons are, as you say, "roughly representative of the *total reasons*" that God has to allow evil. And for all we know, some of the as-yet-unknown reasons lodged deep in the icy, dark depths of that divine iceberg could be soul-destroying for finite creatures.

Justin: Well, right, so, just as nearly every action we can take has reasons in support of it and reasons against it, God might have reasons we know about that motivate his actions that are soul-making and others that we are ignorant of that are soul-destroying and that motivate God to avoid certain actions.

The crux of the issue is that, given that we have no reason to think that the moral reasons we know of are representative of the whole of moral reasons, we are in no position to say one doesn't cancel out the other. If we're to endorse this skeptical attitude about moral reasons to avoid key inferences in arguments from evil, then it needs to be consistent and recognize that all we are doing is punting to mystery. On the other hand, atheism renders the facts about suffering identified in this chapter a matter of common course.

Randal: Sorry Justin, but it seems to me that you're the one punting to mystery here. What you neglect to observe is that whatever additional reasons God may have must be *consistent with the reasons already revealed.* The theist believes God is maximally good and wise and that God always acts in a way consistent with the end of eventually achieving the maximum shalom or wellness for his creatures. This means that whatever other reasons for allowing evil may be hidden in the dark depths, they must be in accord with God's unwavering desire for his creatures to flourish. And with that fact the skeptical worries you've raised melt like, well, an iceberg in the tropics.

Justin: I agree fully with that. I'm not suggesting the possibility that God has soul-destroying behavior that she engages in. I'm suggesting just the opposite. Just like with human decision makers, there are going to be reasons for or against God doing any particular action. For all we know, from God's perspective, the soul-making reasons that we mere humans know of may be cancelled out by soul-destroying reasons of which we are ignorant and of which God knows all too well. If the view about our ignorance compared to God's is correct, none of us are in a position to say this is unlikely.

Randal: There you go punting to mystery again with your "for all we know" speculations. So if we're going to play that game, then here's another one: for all we know, we're brains in vats being fed a matrix of manufactured experience of an external world that doesn't really exist. After all, if we *were* brains in vats we wouldn't be able to tell that we are. So perhaps you want to worry about that too?

Justin: Remember, *you're* the one (not me) who seems willing to appeal to this "for all we know" skepticism of God's potentially hidden reasons. You've done this in an attempt to avoid the thrust of my arguments throughout this entire conversation. I've argued that you've failed to consider consistently the implications on your end.

You'll no doubt disagree. But I think we may have hit the last dead-end in our conversation.

Randal: You're right, I disagree. The fact is that *you're the one* who needs to come to terms with the fact that your ad hoc atheistic parries are futile when contrasted with my intellectually superior theistic swordplay. Ahem, and now as I have your back against the wall once again, alas we find the chapter coming to a close!

Justin: Here I was thinking the Monty Python ending would never come!

Randal: Indeed! But you fought bravely Black Knight, even if I've left you hopping on one leg!

And, as you've observed, we have indeed hit the last dead-end in the road. But I'll give you this: it sure has been a fun drive—or fight (I think I've lost track of the metaphor)!

CONCLUSION

Once upon a time an atheist and a Christian walked into a bar. The dialogue that ensued was ingenuous and provocative and filled the many pages of a future bestseller and philosophical classic. And so things went, page after page, as these two brilliant minds plundered the depths of the universe in a take-no-prisoners debate over the existence of the creator and sustainer of all things, aka, God.

Whew!

But all good things must come to an end and, alas, that includes even that amazing conversation between that atheist and that Christian at the bar. After many pages and arguments, debates and disagreements, a goblet of barley wine and a cocktail with a little umbrella, their intellectual energies spent, and their emotional reserves emptied, Randal and Justin *finally* decided it was time to offer their parting words to you, the reader. And so, as the lights in the bar are dimmed and the credits begin to roll, we turn to heed their reflections in the same order in which they began.

RANDAL'S FINAL PARTING WORD

Okay, I guess since I started the book off I might as well kick off the conclusion as well. And I want to begin with a story.

As that story goes, the eighteenth-century French atheist Denis Diderot so irritated Catherine the Great with his godless proselytizing of Russian elites that she invited the brilliant mathematician Leonhard Euler to the royal court to prove the existence of God. And so, at the royal behest, both Euler and Diderot appeared before the queen and her assembled guests. Euler the mathematician came prepared with an algebraic equation, which he promptly recited and then declared, "Hence, God exists! Reply!" Alas, Diderot had no reply, for he did not even understand the equation, and so the atheist ceded the debate and retreated in humiliation back to Paris.[1]

I like that story for a few reasons. And contrary to what you might think, the fact that Euler the theist appears to win the debate is not one of them.

The first reason I like that story is because it effectively highlights the nature of *expectations* about debates. When it comes to debates about God's existence, people have often looked for irrefutable deductive arguments, something along the lines of a mathematical proof that can leave one's opponent defeated and humiliated beneath the weight of unanswerable evidence. But very rarely, if ever, are matters of debate really like that. Whether the issue under debate involves politics, ethics, history, economics, or theology and the philosophy of religion, what we discover time and again is that reasonable people regularly find themselves coming down on opposite sides of an issue.

In my estimation, the back-and-forth that Justin and I have engaged in provides a reflection of that fact. Wherever your sympathies may lie, I hope our conversation has illustrated the fact that there is indeed room for reasonable and irenic disagreement on the great and daunting question of God's existence. This is not a topic amenable to simple proofs.

And that brings me to the second reason I like the Euler story. At first glance, Euler comes out looking like the hero who won the debate while Diderot shuffles away in shame as the disgraced loser. But look closer and things appear rather different. How so? Well, note that Euler supposedly carried the day by presenting an argument that was not even *comprehended* by Diderot, let alone the audience gathered to hear the exchange. In other words, folks ended up learning precisely *nothing* about the evidence for or against God's existence. All they learned was that Euler was apparently good at math (and not so good at communication).

That reflects a common problem in debates on contentious topics, the problem that people focus on posturing to save face and rhetorical strategies to win an argument. Needless to say, all this comes at the expense of clear, accessible, and *vulnerable* interaction that can help illumine the reasons for and against the various views at play.

With this in mind, Justin and I have both undertaken this conversation with a commitment not simply to winning a debate, but rather to presenting clear and accessible arguments for our sides while honestly unpacking the deep divisions that remain between us. Whether either of us ought to retreat in humiliation back to Paris, I suppose is for the reader to decide. But at least we've stated our reasons for belief and disbelief in a manner clearer, more accessible, and more vulnerable than Euler ever did.

Okay, there is *one* more reason that I like the Euler story. While I don't care so much that Euler seemed to win the debate, I do like the fact that *theism* appears to win the debate. For all the limitations of that ill-fated exchange, it seems to me that most spectators would have come away with a perspective that led them closer to the truth rather than farther from it. In other words, they were left with a witness to the intellectual strength and truth of theism. Since I count the existence of God to be a matter both true and important, I consider this conclusion to be a good thing, whatever else one might say of the limitations of the exchange. Truth is important, and above all I want people to find it.

Like Euler, my own defense undoubtedly has its weak points. (And were the great mathematician here, I'm sure he'd be happy to point some of them out.) But for all those limitations, I believe theism is true. And just as that audience likely left that hall with a deepened faith in God, so I hope it is for those who leave this book. For those theists who picked up this book, I hope the result of having weathered the conversation is a stronger, deeper, more confident and worldly wise belief in God now than when you started. And for the atheists who flipped open the cover, I hope you have a new appreciation for the intellectual credibility of theistic, and Christian, belief. And maybe, just maybe, you even have one more important true belief now than when you started.

Pax vobis,
Randal Rauser

JUSTIN'S FINAL PARTING WORD

As you should know by now, the purpose of this book was to have a lively dialogue on the issue of whether or not there exists a monotheistic God as traditionally defined. However, given the informal, conversational format that we've chosen for ourselves, the flow of our exchange can seem, at times, a bit unusual. I should, however, caution readers not to mistake this feature for a bug. We purposefully tossed the proverbial playbook to the side and pointed our respective collections of arguments in the general direction we wished to go. This is how *real* conversations happen. They're a messy and disorganized back and forth. They backtrack and sometimes require correction. They don't always permit you to say everything that you might have hoped to get out. They are, however, a rewarding experience when done with a worthy dialogue partner. Yes, we've each fallen clear off our proper course more than a few times, tumbled down old rabbit trails, chased a few red herrings, and hit a few dead-ends, but we always managed to get ourselves back to the core question of the existence of God.

The question of the existence of God can be, and often is, seen as a rather divisive topic to explore. The way one answers the question can dramatically affect how one sees the world and one's place in it. If past experience is to have anything to say about any evangelistic prospects, willing spectators who were previously quite confident in their positions are unlikely to have been swayed much from their initial positions. This, I suspect, may have less to do with the quality of arguments found along the way and more to do with interesting psychological facts regarding how beliefs are formed and held onto. We are imperfect inference machines with brains clustered with biases of which we are largely unaware.

Ultimately, it matters little to me that readers are unlikely to have been swayed in either direction. I did not begin this dialogue with a primary goal of acquiring new notches on my atheistic belt (not to be confused with the Bible Belt of the continental United States). I began this project because I love the dialogue, the concepts involved, and the joy I get with exploring the mechanics of how arguments interact.

In my case for atheism, I presented three arguments. The first argument, if you recall, appealed to the fact that many devout theists disagree in important ways on questions as important as how best to relate to God and what kind of lives God wishes us to live. I concluded that this fact is one that we should find relatively surprising if we assume theism to be true. Why would God allow such disagreement to persist among those with whom she wishes to have a relationship?

In my second argument, I brought our attention to the fact that the universe in which we live is almost entirely a deathtrap for the lifeforms we know to exist. If God exists and has created the universe, she has created the universe at least in part as a place for us to interact with each other and navigate our lives as moral agents. I've argued that if atheism is true, the hostility to life of the universe is no surprise at all, while, on theism, our expectations look very different. On theism, we'd expect the universe not to be so threatening to our lives.

For my third argument, I presented the fact of evolution as evidence against theism. Assuming life exists and atheism is true, Darwinian evolution would be one of the few plausible options available to a blind, indifferent universe. And yet theism gives us reasons that don't exist on atheism to think that the suffering and death, which is intrinsic to the process of natural selection, wouldn't be a plausible choice for a morally perfect, omnipotent being to bring about the variety of creatures we now observe.

These arguments were all inductive arguments. They were never intended to be a deductive nail in the coffin of classical theism. I was not expecting to add yet another idol to the overpopulated graveyard of ancient gods or even to injure the rationality of theistic belief. Rather, I was merely presenting some reasons why an atheist could be rational in their judgment that atheism is true.

The arguments in this book are by no means exhaustive of the arguments that are out there, but I do believe they offer a great place to start exploring the issue of the existence of God.

In reason,
Justin Schieber

NOTES

INTRODUCTION

1. I devoted an entire book—*Is the Atheist My Neighbor? Rethinking Christian Attitudes toward Atheism* (Eugene, OR: Cascade, 2015)—to rebutting this popular idea.

2. Randal Rauser, *The Swedish Atheist, the Scuba Diver, and Other Apologetic Rabbit Trails* (Downers Grove, IL: InterVarsity, 2012), p. 12.

CHAPTER 1: WHY GOD MATTERS

1. Jonathan Rauch, "Let It Be," *The Atlantic*, May 2003, http://www.the atlantic.com/magazine/archive/2003/05/let-it-be/302726/ (accessed June 13, 2016).

2. John Vitti, "Weekend at Burnsie's," *The Simpsons*, season 13, episode 16, directed by Michael Marcantel, first aired April 7, 2002, Fox.

3. Mt. 7:7 (NRSV).

4. Acts 17:24–25 (NIV).

5. See, Stephen Law, "The Evil-God Challenge," *Religious Studies* 46, no. 3 (September 2010): 353–73.

6. J. L. Schellenberg, *The Wisdom to Doubt: A Justification for Religious Skepticism* (Ithaca, NY: Cornell University Press, 2007), p. 197.

7. One might also question this assumption. After all, if God is perfect, why think she would be likely to create anything external to herself?

See, Herman Philipse, *God in the Age of Science? A Critique of Religious Reason* (Oxford: Oxford University Press, 2012), p. 149.

8. Thomas Nagel, *The Last Word* (Oxford: Oxford University Press, 1997), pp. 130–31.

9. Christopher Hitchens and Peter Hitchens, "Hitchens v Hitchens Debate," April 3, 2008, Hauerstein Center, YouTube video, 34:30, Jun 15, 2011, https://www .youtube.com/watch?v=ngjQs_QjSwc.

10. This master/slave rhetoric, while punchy, does not apply to mere theism. That's not to say it isn't a proper description of some popular religious forms of theism that call for complete, unquestioning submission. Theism, however, need not entail a demand for this sheeplike, submissive attitude from believers.

11. Sarah Laskow, "Found: A Creepy Note from a House's Former Inhabitant," *Atlas Obscura*, March 16, 2016, http://www.atlasobscura.com/articles/found-a-creepy-note-from-a-new-houses-former-inhabitant?utm_source=twitter&utm_medium=atlas-page (accessed April 25, 2016).

CHAPTER 2: GOD, FAITH, AND TESTIMONY

1. Robert Merrihew Adams, *The Virtue of Faith, and Other Essays in Philosophical Theology* (New York: Oxford University Press, 1987).

2. See, for example, C. Stephen Evans, *Passionate Reason: Making Sense of Kierkegaard's* Philosophical Fragments (Bloomington, IN: Indiana University Press, 1992).

3. Randal Rauser, *You're Not as Crazy as I Think: Dialogue in a World of Loud Voices and Hardened Opinions* (Colorado Springs, CO: Biblica, 2011), p. 39.

4. For further discussion, see, John Vickers, "The Problem of Induction," *Stanford Encyclopedia of Philosophy*, November 15, 2006, http://plato.stanford.edu/entries/induction-problem/ (accessed May 20, 2016).

5. Elliot Sober, *Evidence and Evolution: The Logic Behind the Science* (Cambridge, UK: Cambridge University Press, 2008), p. 136.

CHAPTER 3: THE PROBLEM OF MASSIVE THEOLOGICAL DISAGREEMENT

1. Colin Howson, "Evidence and Confirmation," in *A Companion to the Philosophy of Science*, ed. W. H. Smith (Oxford: Blackwell, 2001), p. 108.

2. Robert A. Pape, *Dying to Win: The Strategic Logic of Suicide Terrorism* (New York: Random House, 2005), p. 4, emphasis added.

3. Ibid.

4. Elliot Sober, "The Design Argument," in *The Blackwell Guide to Philosophy of Religion*, ed. W. E. Mann (Hoboken, NJ: Wiley-Blackwell, 2008), pp. 117–47.

5. For a more robust account of what follows from divine love with respect to meaningful, conscious relationships with God's created finite persons, see, J. L. Schellenberg, *Divine Hiddenness and Human Reason* (Ithaca, NY: Cornell University Press, 1993).

6. Cited in Paul Murray OP, *Aquinas at Prayer: The Bible, Mysticism and Poetry* (London: Continuum, 2013), p. 28.

CHAPTER 4: GOD AND MORAL OBLIGATION

1. Alonzo Fyfe, "A Basic Review of Desirism," *Atheist Ethicist* (blog), December 28, 2011, http://atheistethicist.blogspot.com/2011/12/basic-review-of-desirism .html (accessed June 14, 2016).

2. Cited in Clarence Bauman, *The Sermon on the Mount: The Modern Quest for Its Meaning* (Macon, GA: Mercer University Press, 1985), p. 13n11.

3. Alonzo Fyfe, "What Ought a Person to Do?" *Atheist Ethicist* (blog), March 18, 2008, http://atheistethicist.blogspot.com/2008/03/what-ought-person-to-do .html (accessed June 14, 2016).

4. John Rabe, in *Nanking,* directed by Bill Guttentag (2007; New York: A&E Television Networks, 2008), DVD.

5. C. Stephen Evans, *God and Moral Obligation* (Oxford: Oxford University Press, 2013), p. 15.

6. See, Randal Rauser, "I Want to Give the Baby to God: Three Theses on Devotional Child Killing," (paper presented at the Evangelical Philosophical Society Annual Meeting, Atlanta, Georgia, November 17–19, 2010), http:// randalrauser.com/wp-content/uploads/2010/11/Three-Theses-on-Devotional -Child-Killing.pdf (accessed August 5, 2016).

7. Bertrand Russell, "A Free Man's Worship," in *Why I Am Not a Christian and Other Essays on Religion and Related Subjects* (New York: Touchstone, 1957), p. 107.

8. Cited in David Baggett and Jerry Walls, *Good God: The Theistic Foundations of Morality* (New York: Oxford University Press, 2011), p. 234n35.

9. Paul Babiak and Robert Hare, *Snakes in Suits: When Psychopaths Go to Work* (New York: Harper Collins, 2006).

10. For more on this topic, see an analysis of an online debate between Paul Draper and Alvin Plantinga: Paul Draper, "In Defense of Sensible Naturalism," *The Secular Web,* 2007, http://infidels.org/library/modern/paul_draper/naturalism .html (accessed June 15, 2016).

CHAPTER 5: THE PROBLEM OF THE HOSTILITY OF THE UNIVERSE

1. Here, the word *hostile* refers to the danger that the universe poses to the existence and survival of life forms and is not to be taken literally or to hint at any design or purpose.

2. Philip Plait, *Death from the Skies! These Are the Ways the World Will End . . .* (New York: Viking, 2008), p. 1.

3. The core of the hostility argument originates with Jeffrey Jay Lowder.

Lowder uses the argument in an online debate: "DEBATE: Naturalism or Christian Theism? Jeff Lowder vs. Kevin Vandergriff," Doubtcast, YouTube video, 9:10, November 21, 2014, https://www.youtube.com/watch?v=BBY-Ze0_nWk.

4. Plait, *Death from the Skies!* p. 3.

5. Cited in Julian Wuerth, *Kant on Mind, Action, and Ethics* (Oxford: Oxford University Press, 2014), p. 332.

6. See, Carl Sagan, *Pale Blue Dot: A Vision of the Human Future in Space* (New York: Ballantine, 1994), chapter 1.

CHAPTER 6: GOD, MATHEMATICS, AND REASON

1. E. P. Wigner, "The Unreasonable Effectiveness of Mathematics in the Natural Sciences," *Communications on Pure and Applied Mathematics* 13, no. 1 (February 1960): 14.

2. All these examples are surveyed in Thomas Koshy, *Fibonacci and Lucas Numbers with Applications* (New York: Wiley-Interscience, 2001), chapter 2.

3. Meandering ratio is calculated by taking to the total length of a river divided by a straight line from its source to its mouth.

4. Hans-Henrik Stolum, "River Meandering as a Self-Organization Process," *Science* 271, no. 5256 (March 22, 1996): 1710–13. Cf. Alfred S. Posamentier and Ingmar Lehmann, *Pi: A Biography of the World's Most Mysterious Number* (Amherst, NY: Prometheus, 2004), p. 139.

5. Daniel McCabe, *Nova: The Great Math Mystery*, DVD, directed by Dan McCabe and Richard Reisz (April 15, 2015; Arlington, VA: PBS, 2015).

6. My description assumes that God is temporal and thus that one can describe the relationship from decree to actualization of that decree in temporal terms (i.e., first God decrees and then God creates). However, many theologians believe God is atemporal. In that case, the priority of decree to its actualization would be understood in terms of logical rather than temporal priority.

7. Todd J. Cooke, "Do Fibonacci Numbers Reveal the Involvement of Geometrical Imperatives or Biological Interactions in Phyllotaxis?" *Botanical Journal of the Linnean Society* 150, no. 1 (January 2006): 3.

8. Philip Ball, *Shapes: Nature's Patterns: A Tapestry in Three Parts* (Oxford: Oxford University Press, 2009), p. 236.

9. Gregory Dawes, *Theism and Explanation* (New York: Routledge, 2009), p. 14.

10. Cited in Peter Collier, *A Most Incomprehensible Thing: Notes Towards a Very Gentle Introduction to the Mathematics of Relativity*, 2nd ed. (Harlow, UK: Incomprehensible Books, 2014), p. 16.

11. See, Alexandra Witze, "Einstein's 'Time Dilation' Prediction Verified," *Scientific American*, September 22, 2014, http://www.scientificamerican.com/article/einsteins-time-dilation-prediction-verified/ (accessed May 10, 2016).

CHAPTER 7: EVOLUTION AND THE BIOLOGICAL ROLE OF PAIN

1. Paul Draper, "Evolution and the Problem of Evil," in *Philosophy of Religion: An Anthology*, ed. Louis P. Pojman et al., 3rd ed. (Belmont, CA: Wadsworth Publishing, 1997), p. 221.

2. Robert P. Crease and Charles C. Mann, *The Second Creation: Makers of the Revolution in Twentieth Century Physics*, rev. ed. (New Brunswick, NJ: Rutgers University Press, 1996), p. 9.

3. Paul Draper, "Pain and Pleasure: An Evidential Problem for Theists," *Noûs* 23 (1989): 331–50.

4. Paul Draper, "The Skeptical Theist," in *The Evidential Argument From Evil*, ed. Daniel Howard-Snyder (Bloomington, IN: Indiana University Press, 1996), pp. 175–92.

CONCLUSION

1. See, Simon Singh, *Fermat's Enigma: The Epic Quest to Solve the World's Greatest Mathematical Problem* (New York: Walker, 1997), pp. 76–77.

BIBLIOGRAPHY

Adams, Robert Merrihew. *The Virtue of Faith and Other Essays in Philosophical Theology.* New York: Oxford University Press, 1987.

Babiak, Paul, and Robert Hare. *Snakes in Suits: When Psychopaths Go to Work.* New York: HarperCollins, 2006.

Baggett, David, and Jerry Walls. *Good God: The Theistic Foundations of Morality.* New York: Oxford University Press, 2011.

Ball, Philip. *Shapes: Nature's Patterns: A Tapestry in Three Parts.* Oxford: Oxford University Press, 2009.

Bauman, Clarence. *The Sermon on the Mount: The Modern Quest for Its Meaning.* Macon, GA: Mercer University Press, 1985.

Collier, Peter. *A Most Incomprehensible Thing: Notes Towards a Very Gentle Introduction to the Mathematics of Relativity.* 2nd ed. Harlow, UK: Incomprehensible Books, 2014.

Cooke, Todd J. "Do Fibonacci Numbers Reveal the Involvement of Geometrical Imperatives or Biological Interactions in Phyllotaxis?" *Botanical Journal of the Linnean Society* 150, no. 1 (January 2006): 3–24.

Crease, Robert P., and Charles C. Mann. *The Second Creation: Makers of the Revolution in Twentieth Century Physics.* Rev. ed. New Brunswick, NJ: Rutgers University Press, 1996.

Dawes, Gregory. *Theism and Explanation.* New York: Routledge, 2009.

Draper, Paul. "Evolution and the Problem of Evil." In *Philosophy of Religion: An Anthology,* edited by Louis P. Pojman et al., 219–30. Belmont, CA: Wadsworth Publishing, 1997.

———. "Pain and Pleasure: An Evidential Problem for Theists." *Noûs* 23, no. 3 (June 1989): 331–50.

———. "The Skeptical Theist." In *The Evidential Argument from Evil,* edited by Daniel Howard-Snyder, 175–92. Bloomington, IN: Indiana University Press, 1996.

Evans, C. Stephen. *God and Moral Obligation.* Oxford: Oxford University Press, 2013.

———. *Passionate Reason: Making Sense of Kierkegaard's* Philosophical Fragments. Indiana Series in the Philosophy of Religion. Bloomington, IN: Indiana University Press, 1992.

Hauerstein Center. "Hitchens v Hitchens Debate." YouTube video, 34:30. June 15, 2011. https://www.youtube.com/watch?v=ngjQs_QjSwc.

Koshy, Thomas. *Fibonacci and Lucas Numbers with Applications.* New York: Wiley-Interscience, 2001.

Laskow, Sarah. "Found: A Creepy Note from a House's Former Inhabitant." *Atlas Obscura*, March 16, 2016. http://www.atlasobscura.com/articles/found-a-creepy-note-from-a-new-houses-former-inhabitant?utm_source=twitter&utm_medium=atlas-page (accessed April 25, 2016).

Law, Stephen. "The Evil-God Challenge." *Religious Studies* 46 (2010): 353-373.

McCabe, Daniel. *Nova: The Great Math Mystery.* DVD. Directed by Daniel McCabe and Richard Reisz. April 15, 2015; Arlington, VA: PBS, 2015.

Murray, Paul. *Aquinas at Prayer: The Bible, Mysticism and Poetry.* London: Continuum, 2013.

Nagel, Thomas. *The Last Word.* Oxford University Press, 1997.

Nanking. DVD. Directed by Bill Guttentag. 2007; New York: A&E Television Networks, 2008.

Pape, Robert A. *Dying to Win: The Strategic Logic of Suicide Terrorism.* New York: Random House, 2005.

Philipse, Herman. *God in the Age of Science? A Critique of Religious Reason.* Oxford: Oxford University Press, 2012.

Posamentier, Alfred S. and Ingmar Lehmann. *Pi: A Biography of the World's Most Mysterious Number.* Amherst, NY: Prometheus, 2004.

Rauch, Jonathan. "Let It Be." *The Atlantic*, May, 2003, http://www.theatlantic.com/magazine/archive/2003/05/let-it-be/302726/ (accessed June 13, 2016).

Rauser, Randal. *Is the Atheist My Neighbor? Rethinking Christian Attitudes toward Atheism.* Eugene, OR: Cascade, 2015.

———. "I Want to Give the Baby to God: Three Theses on Devotional Child Killing." Paper presented at the Evangelical Philosophical Society Annual Meeting, Atlanta, Georgia, November 17–19, 2010.

———. *The Swedish Atheist, the Scuba Diver, and Other Apologetic Rabbit Trails.* Downers Grove, IL: InterVarsity, 2012.

———. *You're Not as Crazy as I Think: Dialogue in a World of Loud Voices and Hardened Opinions.* Colorado Springs, CO: Biblica, 2011.

Russell, Bertrand. *Why I Am Not a Christian and Other Essays on Religion and Related Subjects.* New York: Touchstone, 1957.

Sagan, Carl. *Pale Blue Dot: A Vision of the Human Future in Space.* New York: Ballantine, 1994.

Schellenberg, J. L. *The Wisdom to Doubt: A Justification for Religious Skepticism.* Ithaca, NY: Cornell University Press, 2007.

Singh, Simon. *Fermat's Enigma: The Epic Quest to Solve the World's Greatest Mathematical Problem.* New York: Walker, 1997.

Sober, Elliot. "The Design Argument." In *The Blackwell Guide to Philosophy of Religion,* edited by W. E. Mann, 117–47. Hoboken, NJ: Wiley-Blackwell, 2008.

———. *Evidence and Evolution: The Logic behind the Science.* Cambridge: Cambridge University Press, 2008.

Stolum, Hans-Henrik. "River Meandering as a Self-Organization Process." *Science* 271, no. 5256 (March 22, 1996): 1710–13.

Vickers, John. "The Problem of Induction." *Stanford Encyclopedia of Philosophy.* http://plato.stanford.edu/entries/induction-problem/ (accessed May 20, 2016).

Wigner, E. P. "The Unreasonable Effectiveness of Mathematics in the Natural Sciences." *Communications on Pure and Applied Mathematics* 13, no. 1 (February 1960): 1–14.

Witze, Alexandra. "Einstein's 'Time Dilation' Prediction Verified." *Scientific American,* September 22, 2014. http://www.scientificamerican.com/article/einsteins-time-dilation-prediction-verified/ (accessed May 10, 2016).

Wuerth, Julian. *Kant on Mind, Action, and Ethics.* Oxford: Oxford University Press, 2014.

INDEX